BLACK
OPS

ACKNOWLEDGEMENTS

The author owes a debt of gratitude to those members of the international intelligence community who assisted his research, among them Lionel Lowe, Sigismund Payne Best, Euan Rabagliati, Ursula Kuczynski, Len Beurton, Tommy Robertson, Bill Cavendish-Bentinck, Oleg Gordievsky, Michael Bogdanov, Cecil Phillips; Peter Wright, Jim Skardon, Barrie Penrose, Meredith Gardner, Robert Lamphere, Gunter Peis, Michael Ryde, Peter Ramsbotham, Jurgen Kuczynski, Arthur Martin, Rodney Dennys, Charles Seymour, Ray Batvinis, Dan Meinertzhagen, Dan Mulvenna, Russell Lee, BRUTUS, GARBO, TATE, TRICYCLE, ZIGZAG and BRONX.

THIS IS A WELBECK BOOK

Design copyright © Welbeck Non-fiction Limited 2020
Text copyright © Welbeck Non-fiction Limited 2020

This edition published in 2020 by Welbeck
An imprint of the Welbeck Publishing Group
20 Mortimer Street
London
W1T 3JW

Printed in Dubai

A CIP catalogue for this book is available from the British Library

ISBN: 978 0 233 00624 6

BLACK OPS

SECRET MILITARY OPERATIONS FROM
1914 TO THE PRESENT

NIGEL WEST

WELBECK

CONTENTS

INTRODUCTION

Black Ops is the term used, mainly within the intelligence community, to categorize deniable, state-sponsored clandestine operations. It can also be taken to include some of the much wider activities undertaken by conventional espionage agencies that, in an age of disclosure and semi-transparency, embrace the other disciplines of strategic deception, covert action, cyber warfare and even assassination.

While the orthodox functions of intelligence collection and analysis are the obvious roles for security and intelligence agencies, their intrinsic secrecy, and experience in the field, make them obvious candidates when the need arises for a more direct intervention. Very often this irregular requirement reflects the culture of the country or administration involved. For example, successive Russian organizations, from the days of the tsar's dreaded security service, the Okhrana, have indulged in repressive activities more akin to a secret police than a legitimate security apparatus. Likewise, the Soviet Cheka, OGPU, NKVD, KGB and now the SVR and FSB have inherited an increasingly bloody reputation for carrying out the Kremlin's dirty work. In contrast, the rather saintly MI6 Chief Maurice Oldfield declared himself aghast when his Foreign Secretary, Dr David Owen, casually asked in 1977 if the Ugandan despot Idi Amin could be "bumped off".

It often takes a war to concentrate minds and

act as the catalyst for staid institutions to adopt new and perhaps distasteful tactics. In July 1940 a secret government department, Special Operations Executive (SOE), was created to carry out sabotage in enemy-occupied territory and foment resistance to the Nazis. These tasks were clearly beyond the remit and experience of the venerable Secret Intelligence Service (SIS), known since 1939 by the military intelligence cover designation of MI6. In truth, MI6 had for the previous 20 years been nothing more than a liaison conduit to convey confidential information from Allied and neutral countries. Local representatives, operating under the semi-transparent cover of Passport Control Officers (PCOs) had been declared to their hosts, even in Berlin during the Nazi era, and behaved as a back-channel to Whitehall, never contemplating any activity that might offend the country concerned.

For this reason, during the inter-war period, MI6 came to be regarded as a rather passive organization, reluctant to engage in aggressive operations or indulge in counter-intelligence schemes designed to outwit potential adversaries in Nazi Germany or the Soviet Union. This reluctance to take risks, or become involved in political controversy, may have stemmed from MI6's perceived failures during the ambassadors' plot in August 1918 (see pages 16–19), but the net result was MI6's perceived poor standing, and a distinct hesitancy on the part of its principal clients, the military services, to take much notice of the agency's supposedly valuable "CX" bulletins (intelligence reports).

When a clear need arose, in May 1935, to acquire precise figures on the strength of the Luftwaffe, MI6 deliberately avoided the issue and attempted to conceal the true statistics from Prime Minister Stanley Baldwin for fear of venturing into a febrile public debate. Indeed, when MI6 finally produced really valuable intelligence, derived from intercepted German wireless communications, it was largely ignored by the designated recipients in the armed services because the material, circulated under the codename BONIFACE (a false source cover story to protect its true origins), was dismissed as likely to be as unreliable as MI6's usual CX reporting.

During the first year of the Second World War MI6's reputation was at such a low ebb that even Sir Sam Hoare, who had served in Russia for MI6 during the Great War, sent home his local station commander as soon as he reached Madrid. Hoare rejected Colonel Edward de Renzy-Martin, a distinguished and highly decorated MI6 officer, leaving the embassy wholly reliant on the naval attaché to conduct routine intelligence duties. The situation was even worse across much of the rest of Europe as Blitzkrieg had closed down the PCOs before any stay-behind networks could be planned or implemented.

The separation between intelligence collection and analysis on the one hand, and sabotage on the other, became a model that would be followed by the Americans who, when starting from scratch, deliberately split the Office of Strategic Services (OSS) into Secret Intelligence and Special Operations. This mirror construction had already been reflected by the German Abwehr, which had separated Abteilung I, responsible for intelligence reporting, from Abteilung II which trained saboteurs, and the counter-intelligence branch, Abteilung III. Thus the role of "Black Ops" became institutionalized.

Nigel West

PART 1

THE FIRST WORLD WAR

01. CARL HANS LODY

THE FIRST GERMAN SPY

UNDER AMERICAN ALIAS

A 37-year-old lieutenant in the Seewehr, the German 2nd Naval Reserve, Carl Hans Lody arrived in Newcastle from Bergen on 27 August 1914 carrying a United States emergency passport identifying him as a tourist, "Charles A. Inglis". While in Bergen he had acquired a certificate of American nationality in the same name.

Upon his arrival in the UK, Lody went straight to Edinburgh, where he stayed a month, first at the North British Hotel, then at lodgings in Drumsheugh Gardens, with occasional absences of a night or two, one to the Ivanhoe Hotel in London's Bloomsbury, and another to Peebles. During his travels he managed to dispose of a small handbag, which was never traced. His activities were funded with £200 in banknotes, English gold and German gold; some of the currency was later traced to a South American named Kinkelin who had left England on 1 August.

While in Scotland, Lody collected newspapers, and he was found to have accumulated 22 in all. He also communicated with Stockholm in a telegraphic code and sent letters to the same address written in German containing spy reports *en clair* but directed in the text to "Stammer, Courbierestrasse, Berlin", and also to other addresses, signing himself "Charles", "Lody" and "Nazi". However, from 4 August 1914 all mail posted to Norway and Sweden had been diverted to Salisbury House in London for examination by the censorship authorities, which had been alerted to a list of suspect addresses. Among them was one in Stockholm to which Lody wired on 20 August, having endorsed the original telegram form as "Charles Inglis". The ostensibly innocuous

ABOVE: Carl Hans Lody. Once married to an American heiress, Lody travelled to England on an authentic U.S. passport.

OPPOSITE: The emergency U.S. passport issued to Lody less than three weeks before his mission.

content had been addressed to Adolf Burchard in Stockholm's Drottingatan and consisted of a wholly inaccurate message confirming the presence of Russian infantry in England. It was read by the official censor, photographed by MI5, and then placed back in the regular mail for onward delivery, in the hope of encouraging further incriminating correspondence that could be intercepted. A few days later, on 8 September, a letter addressed to Charles A. Inglis, c/o Thomas Cook, Edinburgh, was received, but Lody never called for it. There followed two long reports signed "Nazi" of 27 and 30 September, which were retained, prompting instructions for Lody's arrest.

Good only for
six months from date.

EMERGENCY PASSPORT.

THIS PASSPORT IS ISSUED TO

Charles A. Inglis

IN ORDER THAT HE MAY

PROCEED TO Travel in Europe.

Embassy
of the
United States of America,

BERLIN GERMANY

To all to whom these presents shall come, Greeting.

I the undersigned, Ambassador Extraordinary and Plenipotentiary
of the United States of America.

hereby request all whom it may concern to permit

Charles A. Inglis

a Citizen of the United States

safely
and freely to pass and in case of need to give
him all lawful Aid and Protection.

Description

Age 39 Years

Stature 5 Feet 8½ Inches Eng.

Forehead High.

Eyes Blue

Nose Straight, medium.

Mouth Medium, straight.

Chin Firm medium

Hair Dark

Complexion Light

Face Long.

Given under my hand and the
Seal of the Embassy of the
United States
at Berlin
the 4th day of August.
in the year 1914 and of the
Independence of the United States
the one hundred and 39th

Signature of the Bearer

Charles A. Inglis

01572

ABDUL HAMID, TURKEY'S DEPOSED SULTAN, REAPPEARS ON THE SCENE

The Daily Mirror

CERTIFIED CIRCULATION LARGER THAN ANY OTHER PICTURE PAPER IN THE WORLD

No. 3,548. | Registered at the G.P.O. as a Newspaper. | TUESDAY, MARCH 9, 1915 | 16 PAGES. | One Halfpenny.

GERMAN DIPLOMAT AS MASTER SPY : MILITARY ATTACHE WHO SENT LODY HERE, PLOTS MORE MISCHIEF IN NEW YORK.

Mrs. Stegler, to whom the discovery of the plot is due.

Captain R. Boy-Ed, Germany's master spy in the States.

Lody on trial in London. — Richard Stegler.

" The same high German officials here who sent Carl Hans Lody to his spy's death in the Tower of London, November 10, 1914, made the arrangements by which I was to have visited England, protected by the fraudulently obtained passport of Richard Madden, an American citizen." This remarkable statement has been made by Richard P. Stegler, a German naval reservist, who has been arrested in the United States in connection with the great spy plot. Stegler says that Captain R. Boy-Ed, military attaché to the German Embassy at Washington and Count Bernstorff's personal representative in New York, asked him to use this false passport to travel to England and secure information regarding the whereabouts of the British Fleet. Mrs. Stegler, it is said, prevailed upon her husband to confess. She is an American.

LEFT: British propagandists in the United States sought to link Lody to the German naval attaché accredited in Washington, DC, Captain Karl Boy-Ed. They succeeded, and he was expelled.

OPPOSITE: Carl Hans Lody at the Guildhall in November 1915, shortly before his execution by firing squad in the Tower of London.

Lody then travelled to Liverpool to join a steamer, the SS *Munster*, to Dublin, accompanied by an American physician, Dr John W. Lea, apparently intending to visit the Royal Navy's base at Queenstown, but on 2 October he was arrested by Detective Inspector Cheeseman of the Royal Irish Constabulary at the Great Southern Hotel in Killarney, where his room was searched and various incriminating notes recording reports of troop movements were found, together with cover addresses in Rome and New York.

Lody was escorted to London for interrogation. When questioned at Scotland Yard by the head of Special Branch, Basil Thomson, he made no significant admissions apart from acknowledging that before the war he had lived in Omaha, Nebraska, where he had been married briefly. He was convicted at his three-day trial at a public court martial held at the Middlesex Guildhall, and sentenced to death on 2 November. Lea, who had been travelling on a genuine passport, was released and allowed to return to the United States. Apparently part of Lody's tradecraft had been to cultivate entirely innocent strangers so they could unwittingly provide him with a degree of cover.

At the trial it was asserted that such ostensibly

harmless words as "shall" and "leave" had coded meanings. It was also revealed that Lody had visited England just before the war and had received telegrams in King's Lynn in June and early July under the name of Inglis and of Sideface. Discreet inquiries conducted in Stockholm identified Lody's covert correspondent as a German agent named "K. Leipziger", and an investigation in the United States showed that the real Charles Inglis had deposited his passport with the German Foreign Ministry in Berlin while applying for an extension to his visa, and had been informed that it had been mislaid.

Lody, who was born in Berlin and brought up in Nordhausen, was divorced from his wife Louise Storz, an American heiress, after a short marriage and had worked as an agent for the Hamburg-Amerika Shipping Company. He was the first Nachrichtenabteilung agent (see box, right) of the war to enter Great Britain and had been recruited by Arthur Tapken, with whom he had served in the navy before he had been obliged to retire early on grounds of ill-health. His mission, apparently his second to the United Kingdom, seems to have been confined to general reporting until after the first major sea-battle of the conflict, when he was to report on British naval losses and then move on to a further assignment in the United States.

GERMAN NAVAL INTELLIGENCE

The Imperial German Navy's intelligence staff, the Nachrichtenabteilung, was usually referred to simply as "N". It was the principal organization responsible for the collection of intelligence against Great Britain and the United States. It was headed by Fritz von Prieger, who was assisted by three directors, Arthur Tapken, Walther Isendahl and Paul Ebert, all naval professionals. Based on research conducted after the war in the Admiralty Staff's records, some 120 N agents were sent on missions to Britain, of whom 19 were Dutch, 14 American, and five were women. In 1917, the military branch of the Nachrichtenabteilung became the General Staff's principal analytical resource and was renamed Fremde Heere ("Foreign Armies"). It was headed first by Richard Hentsch and drew its information chiefly from Abteilung IIIb. Although officially dismantled under the terms of the Treaty of Versailles after the war, a skeleton organization remained under cover of a statistical office until it was reinstated as Fremde Heere in 1931.

02. THE AMBASSADORS' PLOT

THE WEST'S ATTEMPT TO ASSASSINATE LENIN

ACE OF SPIES

Officially appointed the "British Agent" in Russia, in the absence of formal diplomatic relations after the Bolshevik revolution in October 1917, Robert Bruce Lockhart was implicated in a scheme, sometimes called "the ambassadors' plot" to assassinate Vladimir Lenin and overthrow the government. Bruce Lockhart was arrested but released when Maxim Litvinov, his counterpart in London, was taken into custody and held in Brixton prison.

Originally, the notorious British spy Sidney Reilly had planned a coup for September 1918, timed to happen as the government's leading commissars were to meet at the Bolshoi Theatre. Entirely coincidentally, in August, a military cadet assassinated Moisei Uritsky, the head of the intelligence service, the Cheka, in Petrograd. In another entirely unconnected incident, Dora Kaplan shot and wounded Lenin as he left a meeting held in a Moscow factory. The government reaction was the "red terror' in which thousands of supposed counter-revolutionaries were arrested and, on 4 September 1918, the British embassy in Petrograd was raided, and the naval attaché, Captain Leslie Cromie, killed as he tried to defend the building from the intruders. In reality, Kaplan had not acted as part of a wider conspiracy; she was shot on 3 December 1918.

In the meantime, Reilly and Bruce Lockhart had schemed with Ernest Boyce of the British Secret Intelligence Service (MI6) and a Latvian, Colonel Edouard Berzin, to organize a counter-revolution, but Berzin betrayed the plan. The prolonged Bolshevik revenge, wreaked by Feliks Dzerzhinsky,

included a raid on the office of Colonel Henri de Vertement, the senior French intelligence officer in Moscow, on 29 August 1918, which he only narrowly escaped, although his American counterpart, Xenophon Kalamatiano, was caught in September 1918 and sentenced to death. Kalamatiano insisted he was simply an innocent businessman, and not the organizer of a network of 36 agents passing information through him to the US Consul-General, Maddin Summers, and in August 1921 was released to return to the United States. He later took up a teaching post in the languages department of Culver Military Academy in Indiana; he died in November 1923.

Also incriminated were George Hill and Reilly, who both managed to evade the Cheka and escape to England. In the Second World War Lockhart would be appointed director of the Political Warfare Executive, and he died at the age of 70 in 1983.

OPPOSITE: Sigmund Rosenblum AKA Sidney Reilly. An adventurer and bigamist from Odessa, Reilly joined MI6 in March 1918.

ABOVE: Reilly's target was the revolutionary Vladimir Ulyanov, who had lived in London and Zurich before his return to Russia in April 1917 as Vladimir Lenin.

THE
CHEKA

Created by Feliks Dzerzhinsky in December 1917, the Cheka became "the sword and shield" of the Communist Party of the Soviet Union and the foundation of subsequent organizations, including the OGPU, NKVD, KGB and SVR. Even today, the greatest compliment paid to a Russian intelligence officer is to be referred to as "a true Chekist". The professional tradecraft developed and refined by the Cheka was based on the years of experience leading a clandestine life that had been forced on the Bolsheviks, who were obliged to adopt noms

ABOVE: The Russian Civil War was marked by appalling atrocities, often committed by the Reds but blamed on their White adversaries and their foreign troops.

de guerre such as Lenin, Stalin and Trotsky, and to live under the rules of *konspiratsia* (see page 202). The creation of insulated, cell-like structures for networks, compartmented to avoid compromise, and the employment of *duboks* (dead-drops) to pass sensitive communications, would become standard practice for the self-preservation of individual agents.

03. THE ZIMMERMANN TELEGRAM

AN INTERCEPTED TELEGRAM FROM BERLIN
TO MEXICO BROUGHT THE UNITED STATES
INTO THE FIRST WORLD WAR

ROOM 40 CODEBREAKERS

On 16 January 1917, the German foreign minister, Arthur Zimmermann, sent a secret two-part telegram to his ambassador in Washington, DC, Count Johann Bernstorff. In the absence of any German transatlantic cables, it was delivered to the U.S. embassy in Berlin for transmission on a State Department channel, the American cable via Copenhagen and London. The U.S. administration had given its permission for the Germans to use the American communications system in the mistaken belief that the German traffic was supporting peace negotiations.

The cipher employed was a new one, designated 7500. This had replaced the German Foreign Ministry's earlier 13040 code. Bernstorff's 7500 codebook had been delivered to him by a submarine, *U55*, in November 1916. The first part of the message amounted to 850 groups of letters, and the second was 150 groups. Both were decrypted upon delivery on 1 January by the German embassy's staff of seven cipher clerks, who then reciphered the entire text in the older 13040 code for onward transmission by Western Union to Mexico, at a cost of $85. This had to be done because the minister, Heinrich von Eckardt, did not possess a copy of the new 7500 cipher.

The full text (see right) announced an intention by the Germans to engage in U-boat warfare on 1 February and asked the German ambassador in Mexico City to approach his host government with an offer of support if it attacked the U.S. to recover "lost territory in Texas, New Mexico and Arizona".

ABOVE: Foreign Minister Arthur Zimmermann was embarrassed by the disclosure of his cable, but admitted its authenticity.

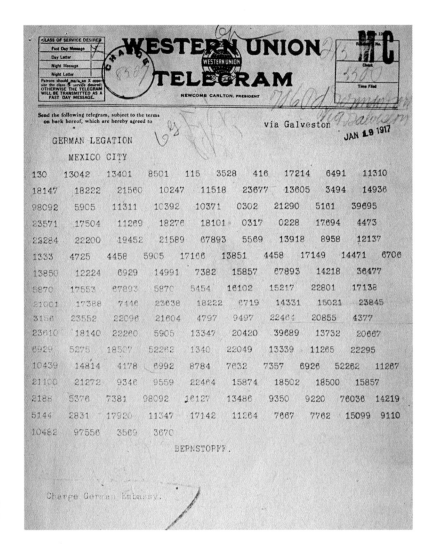

RIGHT: A portion of the
Zimmermann Telegram
that was decrypted by the
British Naval Intelligence
codebreakers.

BERLIN TO WASHINGTON W.158
16 JANUARY 1917

MOST SECRET FOR YOUR EXCELLENCY'S PERSONAL INFORMATION AND TO BE HANDED TO THE IMPERIAL MINISTER IN [?] MEXICO WITH... BY A SAFE ROUTE. WE PROPOSE TO BEGIN ON 1 FEBRUARY UNRESTRICTED SUBMARINE WARFARE IN DOING SO, HOWEVER, WE SHALL ENDEAVOUR TO KEEP AMERICA NEUTRAL.. [?] IF WE SHOULD NOT [succeed in doing so] WE PROPOSE TO [?Mexico] AN ALLIANCE UPON THE FOLLOWING BASIS: [Joint] CONDUCT OF WAR [Joint] CONCLUSION OF PEACE GENEROUS FINANCIAL SUPPORT AND AN UNDERTAKING ON OUR PART THAT MEXICO IS TO RECONQUER THE LOST TERRITORY IN TEXAS, NEW MEXICO AND ARIZONA. THE SETTLEMENT IN DETAIL IS LEFT TO YOU. YOUR EXCELLENCY SHOULD FOR THE PRESENT INFORM THE PRESIDENT [of Mexico] SECRETLY [that we expect] WAR WITH THE USA [possibly] [...Japan].. [Corrupted sentence meaning "Please tell the President"] THAT.. OUR SUBMARINES.. WILL COMPEL ENGLAND TO PEACE WITHIN A FEW MONTHS. ACKNOWLEDGE RECEIPT. ZIMMERMANN

11269 = zu
18276   schalten
15101   ⊙
0317   für den Fall
0228   daß dies
17694   nicht
4473   gelingen
22284   sollte
22200   ⊙
19452   Schlag —en
21589   wir
67893   Mexico.
5569   auf
13918   folgend
8958   grundlage
12137   Bündnis
1333   vor
4725   ⊙
4458   gemeinsam
5905   Krieg
17166   führen
18551   ⊙

4458   gemeinsam
17149.   Friedenschluß.
14471   ⊙
6706   reichlich
13850   finanziell
12224   unterstützung
6929   und
14991   einverständnis
7382   unsererseits.
158(5)7   daß
67893   Mexico.
14218   in
36477   Texas
5870   ⊙
17553   neu
67893   Mexico.
5870   ⊙
5454   AR
16102   IZ
15217   ON
22801   A

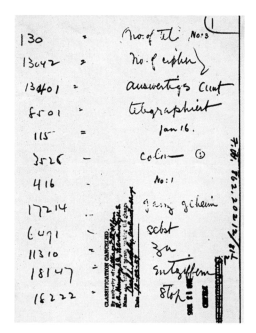

130   =   No. of Tel: No.3
13042   =   No. of cipher
13401   =   auswärtiges amt
8501   =   telegraphiert
115   =   Jan 16.
3528   —   Colm — ⊙
416   No:1
17214   ganz geheim
6491   selbst
11310   zu
18147   entziffern
18222   stop

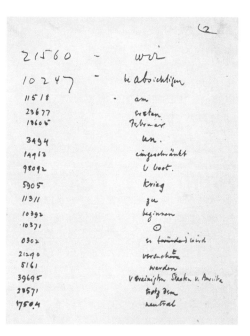

21560   —   wir
10247   —   beabsichtigen
11518   -   am
23677   ersten
18605   Februar
3494   un.
14963   eingeschränkt
98092   U boot.
5905   Krieg
11311   zu
10392   beginnen
10371   ⊙
0302   es (würde) wird
21290   versuchen
5161   werden
39695   V ereinigten Staaten v. Amerika
28571   trotz dem
17504   neutral

The telegram was intercepted in London and decrypted by the British Admiralty's Room 40 (see box on page 25) by the Reverend William Montgomery and Nigel de Grey, who had partially reconstructed the 7500 cipher. The cryptographers' task was made easier by the acquisition from Western Union of a copy of the cable encrypted in the 13040 cipher and by access to a second telegram from Zimmermann, dated 5 February 1917, to his ambassador in Mexico, transmitted on a Swedish channel, to Buenos Aires via Madrid, a route known as the "Swedish roundabout". The second telegram, encrypted in the compromised 13040 cipher, confirmed:

Provided there is no danger of secret being betrayed to USA you are desired without further delay to broach the question of an alliance to the President. The definite conclusion of an alliance, however, is dependent on the outbreak of war between Germany and the USA. The President might even now, on his own account, sound out Japan. If the President declines for fear of subsequent revenge [by the USA] you are empowered to offer him a definite alliance after conclusion of peace provided Mexico succeeds in drawing Japan into the alliance.

The original telegram was finally reconstructed by Room 40 on 19 February 1917 and delivered to the U.S. ambassador, Walter Hines Page, in London on 23 February by the director of naval intelligence, Admiral Reginald Hall, together with a key to the cipher so the American authorities could authenticate it by comparing it with Western Union's version. Secretary of State Robert Lansing showed the offending document to an outraged President Woodrow Wilson on 27 February, and it was handed over to a news agency the following day. Surprisingly, when challenged on 3 March, Count Bernstorff confirmed the authenticity of the

EXPLODING IN HIS HANDS.
—Kirby in the New York *World*.

TOP: American public opinion was outraged by the content of Zimmermann's offer to Mexico.

ABOVE: The 1914 Niagara Falls Conference, which met to avoid war between Mexico and the United States, a peace that was threatened by the Zimmermann Telegram.

OPPOSITE: The original, encrypted text of the Zimmermann Telegram as delivered to the German ambassador in Mexico.

PREPARING OFFICE WILL INDICATE WHETHER

Collect
Charge Department
OR
Charge to
$

TELEGRAM SENT.

Department of State,

Washington,

-2-

to him the substance of the German note and state that it is probable that the contents of this note will be made public in the United States immediately and suggest as your personal opinion that it might be well for the Mexican Government to make some comment.

~~CONFIDENTIAL~~. MERELY FOR YOUR GUIDANCE. The Department does not feel that it can properly withhold from the public the text of this German message. Its publication, however, may cause great consternation and it is possible, unfortunately, that, with the intense feeling aroused, there may be included a degree of uncertainty in regard to the attitude of Mexico unless the Mexican Government can make some statement which might be published simultaneously tending to show their disinterestedness.

Polk
Acting

VFLP/H

CLASSIFICATION CANCELED Authority: letter of 1-8-58 from W. H. Anderson, State Dept.
By R. L. Heise Date 5-28-64

Enciphered by ....

Sent by operator .... *M.*, ..., *191* , ...

Index Bu.—No. 50.

ABOVE: Frank Polk of the U.S. State Department advises his ambassador in Mexico, Henry Fletcher, of imminent "consternation".

ABOVE: Delegates at the Niagara Falls Conference convened to prevent war between the United States and Mexico during Mexico's revolution, when both countries had severed diplomatic relations.

telegram, and as a direct consequence, President Wilson told Congress on 6 April 1917 that America's neutrality would cease.

The fact that the British had intercepted and read the communication was of some sensitivity, so a cover story was fabricated to assuage American sensibilities and create the pretence that the same message had been duplicated on other routes, the Swedish transatlantic cable from Stockholm and the German radio link between Nauen and Sayville, Long Island. To conceal the role played by Room 40, a tale was circulated that the Admiralty had recovered a copy of the 13040 codebook from a captured German agent, Wilhelm Wassmuss, who had been detained at the German consulate in Bushehr earlier in the war.

Embarrassed, Zimmermann expressed his complete confidence in the integrity of his "absolutely secret code" and described the incident as an "act of treachery – one may assume it to have been such", which "appears to have been perpetrated on U.S. territory". His opinion changed after Bernstorff returned from Berlin, having been withdrawn from Washington on 9 February. "Various indications suggest the treachery was committed in Mexico," he claimed on 29 March, prompting Eckardt to protest that only he and his trusted secretary Magnus had handled the telegram and that it was more likely that the leak had occurred in Washington. Dr Otto Göppert, the expert called in to investigate, agreed, concluding that the "betrayal had resulted from American not British action... possibly by the treachery or carelessness of some member of the chancery staff in Washington."

ROOM 40

The Royal Navy's Room 40 was a codebreaking operation staffed by a hand-picked group of academics who proved their cryptanalytic skills by solving many of the enemy's cipher systems, including the German Foreign Ministry's diplomatic code, a coup that would have the severest consequences for Berlin.

04. MATA HARI

DANCER, SPY, DOUBLE AGENT?

FEMME FATALE

Mata Hari, the stage name of Margaretha MacLeod, who performed as a provocatively exotic dancer from the East Indies has become synonymous with glamorous espionage. There is little doubt that she was an amateur German spy in the First World War, but it is possible that she may have been a double agent too.

Margaretha MacLeod arrived at Folkestone on 3 December 1915, on a journey from 16 Niewe Uitleg in The Hague, where she had been since the outbreak of war, on the way to her home at 11 rue Windsor, in Neuilly. When questioned, she claimed to have previously landed at Tilbury on 30 November and after she had been searched she was allowed to continue to France. She had chosen this very inconvenient itinerary, from the neutral Netherlands to Paris, because the German front line made the more direct route impossible.

In fact, on 27 November she had been granted a transit visa to travel from the Netherlands to France via England. She was detained overnight in Folkestone on 3 December when she tried to catch the ferry to Dieppe. She was interviewed by Captain S.S. Dillon, who described her as "handsome, bold... well and fashionably dressed" in a costume with "raccoon fur trimming and hat to match", and he concluded that, "Although she had good answers to every question, she impressed me very unfavourably, but after having her very carefully searched and finding nothing, I considered I hadn't enough grounds to refuse her embarkation."

RIGHT: Mata Hari at the height of her fame, attending the races in 1911 while on a tour of Europe.

ABOVE: Captain Georges Ladoux of the French Deuxieme Bureau.

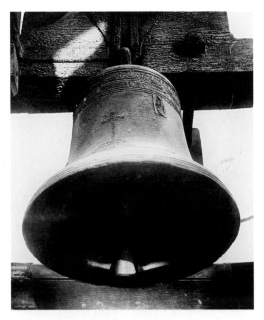

ABOVE: The Death Bell, which tolled at 5.00 p.m. on 15 October 1917 at Vincennes, as Mata Hari was executed.

She continued her journey on the SS *Arundel*, but as her statements about her future travel seemed contradictory and suspicious, MI5 soon afterwards issued a warning to ports recommending she not be allowed to land again. On 22 February 1916, a further notice declared that "this woman is in Holland. If she comes to this country she should be arrested and sent to Scotland Yard." She had been identified by an informant in The Hague as being in the pay of the German embassy and was thought to be "in relation with highly placed people and during her sojourn in France she made the acquaintance of many French and Belgian officers". In summary, "She is suspected of having been to France on important mission for the Germans."

In April 1916, MacLeod applied to the British consul in Rotterdam for a visa, but was refused, as was her appeal to London, conveyed by the Dutch government. However, on 6 November 1916, en route on the SS *Hollandia* from Vigo in Spain to Rotterdam, she was detained at Falmouth when she was mistaken for Clara Benedix, a notorious German spy from Hamburg thought to be employed by the German consul in Barcelona. She was

escorted to London by Detective Inspector George Grant and lodged in the Savoy Hotel. When she was interviewed by Reginald Drake, Lord Herschell and Scotland Yard's assistant commissioner for crime, Basil Thomson, with the help of an interpreter, the issue of her identity was clarified, but she was not released immediately because of her extraordinary claim to be working against the Germans for Captain Georges Ladoux of the French external military intelligence agency, the Deuxième Bureau.

This assertion was denied by Ladoux in a telegram dated 17 November in which he denounced her as a probable German spy. Apparently unimpressed, Thomson returned her to the Savoy Hotel and she was given permission to travel to Holland, but the Dutch authorities refused her an entry permit so on 1 December she sailed on the SS *Araguaga* from Liverpool to Vigo. During her interrogation, she had denied being Clara Benedix but acknowledged having met the woman while travelling from Madrid to Lisbon, recalling that she had dined with her, together with the local British consul, and shared a railway compartment.

Once back in Spain, MacLeod installed herself in

ABOVE: Mata Hari, the exotic dancer, at the age of thirty. Her riské stage performances captivated audiences across Europe.

BELOW: French military personnel gather at the fortress of Vincennes to witness Mata Hari's execution by firing-squad.

Colonel Joseph Devignes. She then applied for, and was granted, a French visa but, having eventually reached Paris on 3 January 1917, she was arrested on 13 February and charged with espionage. At her trial, held in camera before a military tribunal in July 1917, the prosecution alleged that a German signal from Madrid requesting funds for "Agent H-21" had been intercepted by a radio station on the Eiffel Tower and decrypted; after a day and a half she was convicted by a six-man military tribunal and condemned to death. Three months later, in October 1917, she was executed by firing squad, with her Deuxième Bureau contact, Captain Ladoux, present as a witness. According to her French dossier, she confessed to having passed information to the Germans after she had been recruited by Karl Cramer, the consul in Amsterdam.

Although it does seem that MacLeod did pass information to the Germans, she was never a professional spy. Despite her exotic reputation, her appearance certainly did not impress Thomson, who remarked that "time had a little dimmed the charms of which we had heard so much".

After her conviction, an investigation of her contacts led to the arrest of the cabaret singer Jeanne Druin, who was sentenced to 15 years' hard labour. Another of her friends, Germaine d'Anglemont, was also considered an espionage suspect but was never charged.

the Ritz Hotel in Madrid and made plans to reach the Netherlands overland, via Paris. She also introduced herself to the German military attaché, Major Arnold Kalle, and pretended to accept his invitation to become his agent. Simultaneously, she was also in touch with the French military attaché,

1876

conseil de guerre (3)

BULLETIN N° 1

N° 990
DE LA
NOMENCLATURE GÉNÉRALE.

à classer a *Monsieur le Ministre de la Justice Casier Central*

Date du mandat de dépôt :

—

RENSEIGNEMENTS :

Célibataire

Marié *divorcée*

Veuf

Nombre d'enfants

Signes particuliers :

—

MENTIONS POSTÉRIEURES
À LA
RÉDACTION DU BULLETIN :

Peine expirée le

Amende payée le

Contrainte par corps exé-
cutée le

Timbre de la juridiction
qui a prononcé.

754-468-1916.

La nommée *Zelle, Marguerite, Gertrude, dite Mata Hari* (4)

fils { de *Adam* et de *Antje Vandermeulen* } âgé de *40* ans,

né le *7 Août 1876*, à *Leeuwarden*

arrondissement d *Hollande* département d

Domicile à *Paris 12 Boulevard des Capucines*

Profession *danseuse*

Nationalité *Hollandaise*

a été condamnée *le Vingt-quatre Juillet 1917*

par *jugement contradictoire* (6)

du *3e Conseil de guerre* (7)

à { (8) **Mort** ~~francs d'amende~~ (9) (10) (11) } et aux dépens,

pour *Espionnage, intelligences avec l'ennemi dans le but de favoriser ses entreprises*
commis *1915-1916-1917*

par application
des articles *205 §2, 206 §1 et 2, 64, 69, 269, 133* du Code pénal,
187 du Code de justice militaire.

7 du Code d'Instruction Criminelle

Pour extrait conforme :

Paris, le *20 Août 1917*

Vu au parquet :

Le Greffier,

Le Commissaire du Gouvernement, (12)

NOTA. — Pour les bulletins n°* 1 dressés au casier central, le certifié conforme est donné par l'agent chargé du service, le timbre apposé est celui du Ministère de la justice, et le bulletin est visé par le Directeur des affaires criminelles et des grâces. — Pour les bulletins délivrés par les conseils de guerre, il y a lieu d'indiquer au talon les articles du Code de justice militaire qui ont été appliqués.

(1) Greffe du tribunal civil d   ou casier central.
(2) Année de la naissance en chiffres de 1 centimètre de hauteur.
(3) Mention : «Récidive» (s'il y a lieu).
(4) Juridiction qui a prononcé.
(5) Nom, surnoms et prénoms.
(6) Arrêt ou jugement (mentionner s'il est contra-dictoire ou par défaut).
(7) Juridiction qui a prononcé.

(8) Peine corporelle.
(9) Pénalités accessoires, disciplinaires, etc.
(10) Mention du sursis à l'exécution de la peine (s'il y a lieu).
(11) S'il s'agit d'un arrêt rendu par une juridiction d'appel, mentionner : « Sur appel d'un jugement du tribunal d   , en date du   ».
(12) Qualité de l'officier du ministère public suivant la juridiction qui a prononcé.

ABOVE: The official French government bulletin announcing Mata Hari's death following her conviction on charges of espionage.

05. RICHARD MEINERTZHAGEN

THE ORIGINS OF STRATEGIC DECEPTION

FAKER EXTRAORDINAIRE

Although some of the events Richard Meinertzhagen described in his memoirs did take place, including the deliberate placement of misinformation, it seems that he rather exaggerated his own role in them.

Having been commissioned in the British Army in 1899, Richard Meinertzhagen served in India and Burma before being posted to Mombasa in Kenya as a staff officer with the King's African Rifles. He later served at the War Office and in South Africa, and on the outbreak of war Meinertzhagen was on the intelligence staff of the Indian Expeditionary Force sent to Kenya to capture German East Africa. He later returned to England and was then transferred to the Middle East.

According to his own version of events – supposedly recorded in 78 loose-leaf, typewritten volumes of contemporary diaries lodged at Rhodes House in Oxford – in October 1917, Meinertzhagen, a staff officer working for General Sir Edmund Allenby during the Palestine campaign, perpetrated an ingenious deception scheme. The aim was to persuade the Turks that an imminent offensive was to be concentrated on the town of Gaza, whereas when the attack took place the true objective was Beersheba, which was seized easily because Gaza had been reinforced, leaving the outpost vulnerable. Meinertzhagen's plan was to plant a haversack containing secret documents on an unsuspecting enemy, and this he achieved during an encounter with a Turkish patrol, leaving the bloodstained haversack as though the owner had been wounded. The documents suggested that General Allenby would be on leave at the end of October, but upon his

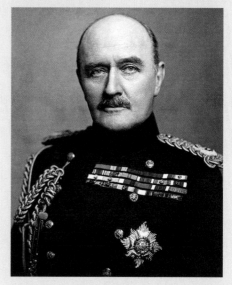

return the following month he would launch a frontal attack on Gaza. According to Meinertzhagen's story, which he published in 1960, the ruse proved highly effective and the capture of Beersheba opened the route to Jerusalem, 100 kilometres (60 miles) away, and broke a stalemate in the Negev Desert that had lasted for six months. However, his tale has been challenged by academics who assert that he was simply a bystander when the haversack deception was perpetrated, and that in any event the key material was disbelieved by the Turks.

Born in 1878, Meinertzhagen was one of the most remarkable polymaths of his era, distinguishing himself as a soldier, scientist, explorer, spy and ornithologist. His bloodthirsty experiences in East Africa, as an officer in the King's African Rifles and a big game hunter, were documented in his diaries, and his *Birds of Arabia* remains a standard textbook on the subject. He also claimed to have battered a man to death with a polo stick for maltreating a pony, and to have killed a German with a knobkerrie that is still preserved in the Tower of London.

By the time his biography, *The Meinertzhagen Mystery*, was published in 2007 by Brian Garfield, several scholars had raised questions about Meinertzhagen's reliability and the authenticity of his claimed encounters with T.E. Lawrence. It was also noted that in 1938 the principal German intelligence officer in the region, Major General Baron Friedrich Kress von Kressenstein, had acknowledged the ruse, but in his memoirs insisted it had been disbelieved.

In 1960, Meinertzhagen published what purported to be his diary entry made on 10 October 1917 at Rafa in Palestine:

OPPOSITE TOP: Richard Meinertzhagen, who claimed in his diary to have deceived the enemy by planting bogus plans.

OPPOSITE: General Edmund Allenby, whose success at Beersheeba in October 1917 ensured the liberation of Palestine.

ABOVE RIGHT: Colonel Meinertzhagen posing with an exhibit acquired for his famous ornithological collection.

Spent today in deceiving the enemy. I have been busy lately compiling a dummy Staff Officer's notebook containing all sorts of nonsense about our plans and difficulties. Today I took it out to the country north-west of Beersheba with a view to passing it on to the enemy without exciting suspicion. I was well mounted and near Girheir I found a Turkish patrol who at once gave chase. I galloped away for a mile or so and then they pulled up, so I stopped, dismounted and had a shot at them at about 600 yards. That was too much for them and they at once resumed the chase, blazing away harmlessly all the time. Now was my chance, and in my effort to mount I loosened my haversack, fieldglasses, water-bottle, dropped my rifle, previously stained with some fresh blood from my horse, and in fact did everything to make them believe I was hit and that my flight was disorderly. They had now approached close enough and I made off, dropping the haversack, which

LEFT: The Natural History Museum at Tring where many of Meinertzhagen's specimens were exhibited.

contained the notebook and various maps, my lunch, etc. I saw one of them stop and pick up the haversack and rifle, so I now went like the wind for home and soon gave them the slip, well satisfied with what I had done and that my deception had been successful. If only they act on the contents of the notebook, we shall do great things.

Supposedly, the haversack contained some additional items intended to enhance credibility: a collection of other plausible correspondence and personal effects, including a letter written by the officer's wife describing the recent birth of his son, and a £20 note.

The main problem with Meinertzhagen's account was that the officer who really undertook the task of delivering the haversack to the enemy had been Captain Arthur C.B. Neate, who died in 1976. He was the sole survivor of the group of British officers who knew about the scheme that had been dreamed up, not by Meinertzhagen, but a staff officer, Colonel James Belgrave, with Brigadier Guy Dawnay. Their proposal had been approved by Generals Louis Bols and Sir Philip Chetwode and endorsed by the Commander-in-Chief, General Allenby.

The story of the deception was first made public in 1920 by Ferdinand Tuohy in *The Secret Corps*, but he concealed Neate's identity by referring to him as "M———." However, in his *Army Diary*, published in 1960, Meinertzhagen inserted himself into Neate's role, apparently confident that those who knew the truth were dead. Belgrave had died in 1918, Dawnay in 1952, Blois in 1930, Chetwode in 1950, and Allenby in 1936. When Neate protested, Meinertzhagen replied that his slightly abbreviated version had omitted mention of Neate's failure – which he said had occurred on 12 September 1917 – to have the material taken by the Turks, and he embellished his tale further by mentioning yet another abortive attempt, supposedly by an Australian officer on 1 October. In this way Meinertzhagen finessed his story and, having retrospectively altered his diary entry, peddled a version that would become accepted, and repeated, by subsequent historians.

Close scrutiny of some of Meinertzhagen's other claims show them to be equally false. Among them were his fanciful tales of having distributed forged banknotes to undermine the economy in German East Africa, of his involvement with a German spy named Friedrich Frank, and of his rescue of the Grand Duchess Tatiana from the Bolsheviks in 1918. Proof of Meinertzhagen's tendency to fabricate his diary was found in an entry for 1917 when he recorded having spotted the Zeppelin *L59* over Sollum in Egypt, whereas the airship was nowhere near the position claimed.

Meinertzhagen's unconventional life, and his highly developed sense of humour, may well have contaminated some aspects of modern military history, but Richard Meinertzhagen was controversial throughout his life, and even afterwards. Upon his death in June 1967 he had bequeathed his collection of 20,000 specimens of birds to the Natural History Museum at Tring in Hertfordshire. However, upon close examination it turned out that many of the items were fraudulently labelled or were stolen. An initial discrepancy relating to the catalogue of finches revealed that a number of the entries had been faked. The impact on ornithology was profound and long-lasting because Meinertzhagen had documented particular species seen at unusual locations and had claimed to have spotted rare or near-extinct birds. His celebrated coup of finding a forest owlet turned out to have been an exhibit purloined from the British Museum. Similarly, he insisted he had found a rare kingfisher in Burma, when the specimen had originated from the Chinese island of Hainan. Meinertzhagen's legacy extended to other museums, which contained his incorrectly tagged birds, including the Museum of Natural History in New York.

ABOVE: A column of the 12th Australian Light Horse approach Beersheeba after Ottoman reinforcements had been sent to Gaza.

06. BLOODY SUNDAY 1920

DUBLIN CASTLE AND THE IRA ATTACK ON
THE COMBINED INTELLIGENCE SERVICE

SUNDAY MORNING MASSACRE

In the space of one morning, the Irish Republican Army (IRA) almost wiped out the Combined Intelligence Service (CIS) that had been formed to undermine the Republican movement.

During the First World War the British Army established a Combined Intelligence Service (CIS), a dedicated unit based at Dublin Castle to operate against the Irish Republican Army (IRA). The CIS was partly drawn from the Dublin District Special Branch and was headed initially by General Sir Henry Tudor, and then by Colonel Ormonde Winter. The CIS's organization was effectively destroyed on Bloody Sunday, 21 November 1920, when IRA gunmen shot 14 CIS officers and killed a further two members of the RIC in a series of coordinated attacks.

A Royal Artillery officer who had served in India, Winter's reputation as an intelligence officer had been established during the Gallipoli campaign when he had interrogated Turkish prisoners with great skill. His appointment to Dublin Castle in May 1920 by the Secretary of State for War, Winston Churchill, was controversial because in 1903 he had been acquitted on a manslaughter charge for killing an Irish youth with an oar when attacked by a gang while boating with a colleague.

TOP: Michael Collins, the charismatic IRA strategist who devised the plan to decapitate the CIS.

RIGHT: Colonel Ormonde Winter, the experienced British intelligence officer drafted in to manage the CIA and infiltrate the IRA.

OPPOSITE: Bodies of the British personnel killed in the massacre being carried aboard the destroyer HMS *Seawolf* for the voyage back to England.

Before the creation of the CIS, the internal structure of the civil and military security apparatus in Ireland was complex because of the parallel nature of the two organizations: one answerable to Scotland Yard in London, which deployed some 60 undercover agents in Ireland, and the other controlled by the Commander-in-Chief, General Sir Nevil Macready, but in reality run by Colonel John Brind and Major Stephen Hill-Dillon. Under Winter's leadership, the CIS opened a training facility in Hounslow to develop a cadre of British intelligence officers dedicated to the task of monitoring and penetrating Irish Republican movement and its political party, Sinn Fein. Another objective was to learn more about Irish secret societies known to be active in the campaign for independence, and their logistical and financial support from the United States. Head agents were assigned particular districts in which to operate, of which there were six in Dublin itself. Colonel Walter Wilson instituted a card-index system for registering suspects and listing candidates for recruitment as informants.

In part as a result of the CIS's activities, the security environment had so improved by September 1920, when agent networks had been created from Drogheda to Arklow, that John Brind had recommended the replacement of the military with the Royal Irish Constabulary (RIC) in recently pacified districts.

On the morning of 21 November, IRA assassins, coordinated by Michael Collins and Richard Mulcahy, called simultaneously at various different addresses across Dublin and murdered 11 British Army officers, one RIC sergeant, two members of the Auxiliary Division and one suspected informant. The gunmen included Peadar Clancy, Tom Cullen, Dick McKee, Liam Tobin, Frank Thornton and Oscar Traynor, and they were armed with revolvers, sledgehammers and a list of targets that had been compiled over several months of observation and information acquired from IRA penetration agents.

The first raid, conducted at nine o'clock by Mick Flanagan, was at 28 Pembroke Street, where Major Charles Dowling, Captain Leonard Price and Captain Brian Keenlyside were shot dead as their rooms were searched and papers removed by one of the gunmen, Andrew Cooney. Mortally wounded, Colonel Hugh Montgomery died three weeks later.

Another officer who was visiting the address, Colonel Wilfred Woodcock, was wounded but survived.

The second raid was on a terraced house at 117 Morehampton Road in Dublin's southern suburb of Donnybrook, where Lieutenant Donald Maclean and a suspected informer, T. J. Smith, were shot dead. The third raid took place a short distance away, at 92 Lower Baggot Street, where Captain William Newberry was shot dead by Bill Stapleton and Joe Leonard. The fourth raid, on 38 Upper Mount Street, resulted in the murder of Lieutenant Peter Ames and Captain George Bennett, who were shot by Vincent Byrne and his companions.

The fifth raid was on 28 Earlsfort Terrace, where a RIC sergeant, John Fitzgerald, was shot twice in the head. The sixth raid was on 22 Lower Mount Street, where Lieutenant Henry Angliss and Lieutenant Charles Peel, both experienced intelligence officers who had served in the north Russia campaign, were

shot by gunmen led by Tom Keogh. Peel survived his wounds. The seventh raid, on 119 Lower Baggot Street, resulted in the death of a military lawyer, Captain Geoffrey Baggallay. The eighth and last raid was on the Gresham Hotel, where a Roman Catholic veterinary surgeon, Captain Patrick McCormack, was shot in his bed in a case of mistaken identity, and Lieutenant Leonard Wilde was killed as he answered a knock on his door.

Three men accused of participating in the raids were arrested and convicted, of whom Patrick Moran and Thomas Whelan were hanged in March 1921, Frank Teeling having escaped from Kilmainham Gaol.

Several CIS officers experienced narrow escapes but, obviously compromised, were quickly moved to the mainland. Ormonde Winter dismantled the CIS in 1922 and was transferred as director of resettlement in the Irish Office until 1924 when he

ABOVE: A French magazine's portrayal of the murder of Michael Collins during an ambush mounted by his republican opponents outside Cork in August 1922.

ABOVE: A wounded British cadet (foreground) and two of the three Irish republicans killed on the Bloody Sunday street battle on 21 November 1920.

ABOVE: Michael Collins, passionately addressing a large crowd in Dublin shortly before his murder in 1922.

retired. He published his memoirs, *Winter's Tale*, in 1955 and died in February 1962 in Worthing, Sussex. Michael Collins would be elected in 1919 to the first Dail to represent the Cork South constituency, but during the subsequent Irish Civil War he was ambushed in August 1922 at a crossroads outside Béal na Bláth near Cork while returning to the city after a tour of the area, driving in an armoured vehicle. Collins was killed by a head wound, but no other details of the incident have ever been disclosed, so the number and names of his assailants, known to be Collins's political opponents, remain unknown.

The liquidation of the Dublin Castle intelligence staff was a ruthless coup-de-main intended to decapitate the British capability to crush the Republican opposition and set a bloody precedent for decisive intervention. The notoriety of the event would remain a significant milestone in the history of irregular warfare and provide some future intelligence professionals, such as Major Hill-Dillon who would join MI6, with an uncomfortable grounding in clandestine operations.

The IRA achieved considerable military success throughout the Troubles by adopting the controversial tactics employed by the Boers during two South African wars, when well-disciplined and motivated Dutch farmers fought against what was generally considered to be the best organized and armed army in the world. By striking at lines of supply and avoiding pitched battles or direct confrontation with numerically superior forces, the elusive Boer commandos were able to mount unexpected raids and then withdraw into the countryside. This meant that they avoided the need to build fixed encampments that could be vulnerable to discovery. An unorthodox strategy, it was dependent on the support of the local civilian population, who concealed caches of weapons and provided food for the lightly armed groups of men. These men would today be recognized as guerrillas, modelled on the marauding, highly mobile cavalry that harassed Napoleon's infantry with such signal success during the Peninsular War. Even the most sporadic raids on reconnaissance patrols, isolated posts and smaller garrisons proved successful. They undermined the enemy's morale, pinning down quite disproportionate numbers of expensive troops and making the conflict unpopular through the alienation of the civilian population by deliberately provoking over-reactions, reprisals and the imposition of other counterproductive policies. All these characteristics would be recognized as the hallmarks of what would later be termed "asymmetric warfare".

07. THE TRUST

THE SOVIET INTELLIGENCE AGENCY'S INFILTRATION OF THE ANTI-BOLSHEVIKS

KONSPIRATSIA

In the aftermath of the Bolshevik revolution the new Soviet intelligence agency, the OGPU, initiated an ingenious operation, which was intended to penetrate, manipulate and ultimately control the regime's opponents. Masterminded by Lenin's Machiavellian intelligence chief, Feliks Dzerzhinsky (see page 18), the Trust purported to be an umbrella organization which acted as a link between émigré groups and a somewhat ephemeral underground resistance network of anti-Communist activists that was allegedly well-established within the Soviet Union.

The Trust had the effect of blunting the impact of the monarchists by dividing the Kremlin's enemies and enabling the Soviet intelligence service, the OGPU, to insert agents into adversarial movements. The operation was directed with such skill that some seasoned anti-Bolshevik operators, among them Boris Savinkov and Sidney Reilly, were lured into traps, and high-profile émigré leaders considered a serious threat to the Communists – including Nikolai Skoblin, General Eugene Miller and General Alexander Kutepov – were abducted off the streets of Paris and liquidated.

The Trust developed a commercial cover, the Moscow Municipal Credit Association, which

TOP RIGHT: Feliks Dzerzhinsky, first head of the dreaded Cheka. Born in Poland, he was steeped in the clandestine life of a revolutionary.

RIGHT: As a revolutionary politician, Boris Savinkov opposed the Bolsheviks but in 1924 would be lured back to Russia where he was arrested.

ABOVE: A massacre of Chekists by kulak farmers at Simbirsk in 1918.

provided a well-funded façade to finance foreign travel and enable nominees to move across frontiers with relative ease. This particular attribute attracted some foreign intelligence agencies, which was part of the OGPU's scheme, but it also engendered some suspicion from sceptics. Among those anxious to exploit the Trust's apparent ease of access was MI6, which channelled money to the organization through Finland. Despite some reservations, the Trust's leadership guaranteed Savinkov safe passage to Moscow so that he could re-establish contact with some of his old supporters. Reilly advised against making such a journey, but Savinkov ignored his pleas and set off for Moscow from Berlin on 10 August 1924. Reilly never saw him again, and a fortnight later the Russian press announced Savinkov's arrest, trial, death sentence and pardon. Savinkov, the bulwark against Communism, had defected to the Bolsheviks.

Reilly was stunned by the news and infuriated, especially when he heard claims that it had been the Trust's influence that had saved Savinkov from execution. Reilly never discovered his mentor's full story because Savinkov committed suicide in May the following year. The loss of Savinkov convinced Reilly that it was now his responsibility to carry on the struggle, and he began a desperate money-raising campaign to finance further armed resistance within the Soviet Union. By the end of 1924 MI6's Chief Hugh Sinclair had distanced his organization from Reilly's activities, but this did not stop Reilly corresponding with Winston Churchill and other senior politicians to gain support for his objectives.

Virtually his only remaining link with MI6 was Ernest Boyce, the long-serving station commander in Helsinki, where he was secretly financing the Trust in exchange for information. Boyce confirmed to Reilly that he had faith in the Trust and introduced him to the Trust's local representative, Alexander Yakushev, one of Boyce's most successful agents, who was also an OGPU official.

ABOVE: The trial of Boris Savinkov in 1925 when he was condemned to death. His sentence was commuted to ten years' imprisonment, which he did not survive.

Yakushev told Reilly exactly what he wanted to hear: the Trust was an enormous organization with influence in every level of the Soviet structure. It enjoyed the protection of certain high Party officials, which virtually guaranteed that its agents could enter and leave the country at will. The Trust was so powerful that even if someone was arrested his release could be arranged with only the minimum of delay. Reilly was intrigued and asked to meet the Trust's leaders. He was told that they occupied such important posts in Moscow that they were unable to leave the capital... but they would be willing to attend a rendezvous with him if he came to Moscow. Incredibly, Reilly swallowed the bait, and on 25 September 1925, when Boyce was in London, Reilly was led across the Finnish border into Russia near Allekul by two Trust couriers. Two days later, Boyce received a postcard from Reilly, postmarked Moscow, but the following week the newspaper *Izvestia* reported that a group of smugglers had been intercepted by the police close to the Finnish border. Three people had been killed and a fourth, a Finnish soldier, was reported a prisoner.

A notice of Reilly's death was included in *The Times* on 15 December 1925, and this prompted further inquiries about his fate. However, nobody was ever able to establish what had happened, although the Trust was later exposed as an elaborate OGPU front. Evidently Dzerzhinsky decided it had been too badly compromised to continue, and in 1927 began liquidating his principal agents. Among them was Alexander Yakushev, who escaped to Finland and admitted his duplicity. Embarrassed by his cupidity, he chose to take early retirement from MI6 and found a job with a commodity firm in Paris run by a wartime colleague, Stephen Alley.

In counter-intelligence circles the Trust is still regarded as a model of a highly successful stratagem. The Soviets later adopted the blueprint for a similar post-war deception in Poland, creating a phoney resistance organization, which would be largely funded by Western intelligence services.

ABOVE: Boris Savinkov was considered a serious threat to the Bolsheviks
who perpetrated an elaborate scheme to tempt him back to Russia.

PART 2

INTER-WAR INTELLIGENCE

08. THE BLACK CHAMBER

THE ORIGINS OF THE AMERICAN CIPHER BUREAU

READING OTHER GENTLEMEN'S MAIL

The American Cipher Bureau was created at the end of the First World War by a gifted cryptographer, Herbert O. Yardley, and was sponsored jointly by the U.S. State Department and the War Department's MI8. Known informally as the Black Chamber, the bureau was a clandestine cryptographic organization that operated under a cover called the Code Compilation Company, in a four-storey brownstone building at 3 East 38th Street in Manhattan. The organization was disbanded in October 1929 by Secretary of State Henry Stimson, and its records were acquired by the U.S. War Department's Signal Intelligence Service.

The bureau enjoyed considerable success, particularly with Spanish diplomatic traffic, and solved some British codes, including one used in a message from the British embassy in Washington, DC, alerting the War Office to Yardley's imminent arrival in London on an official visit in August 1918. Yardley recalled later that he had "consumed a great deal of tea and drank quantities of whisky and soda with various officers in the War Office. They were affable enough and invited me to their clubs. But I received no information."

The most significant American contribution to signals intelligence had been made early in 1916

TOP RIGHT: U.S. State Department seal.

RIGHT: Lieutenant Herbert O. Yardley in June 1917 as he joined the U.S. Army Signal Corps and was assigned to a section designated MI8.

OPPOSITE: Herbert Yardley, who headed the U.S. State Department's "Black Chamber" and broke Japan's diplomatic code. In 1931 he wrote a book about his achievements and lost his security clearance.

13

Alphabetic Frequency Tables

(Truesdell)

Frequency of occurrence in 1,000 letters of text:

Letter	French	German	Italian	Portuguese
A	80	52	117	140
B	6	18	6	6
C	33	31	45	34
D	40	51	31	40
E	197	173	126	142
F	9	21	10	12
G	7	42	17	10
H	6	41	6	10
I	65	81	114	59
J	3	1	*	5
K	*	10	*	
L	49	28	72	32
M	31	20	30	46
N	79	120	66	48
O	57	28	93	110
P	32	8	30	28
Q	12	*	3	16
R	74	69	64	64
S	66	57	49	88
T	65	60	60	43
U	62	51	29	46
V	21	9	20	15
W	*	15		
X	3	*	*	1
Y	2	*	*	1
Z	1	14	12	4

* Occurrence rare, usually in proper names.

Order of Frequency

French

E A N R S I U O L D C P M V Q F G B J Y Z
   T   HX

German

E N I R T S A D G H C L F M B W Z K V P J Q X Y
     U   O

Italian

E A I O L N R T S C D M U V G Z F B Q
              P   H

Portuguese

E A O S R I N M T D C L P Q V F G B J Z X Y
    U   H

14

Graphic Frequency Tables

Frequency of occurrence in 200 letters of text.

French

A	16	1111111111111111
B	2	11
C	6	111111
D	10	1111111111
E	39	111111111111111111111111111111111111111
F	2	11
G	1	1
H	1	1
I	13	1111111111111
J	1	1
K		
L	10	1111111111
M	6	111111
N	16	1111111111111111
O	11	11111111111
P	6	111111
Q	2	11
R	15	111111111111111
S	13	1111111111111
T	13	1111111111111
U	12	111111111111
V	4	1111
W		
X	1	1
Y		
Z		

Italian

A	23	11111111111111111111111
B	1	1
C	9	111111111
D	6	111111
E	25	1111111111111111111111111
F	2	11
G	3	111
H	1	1
I	23	11111111111111111111111
L	14	11111111111111
M	6	111111
N	13	1111111111111
O	19	1111111111111111111
P	6	111111
Q		
R	13	1111111111111
S	10	1111111111
T	12	111111111111
U	6	111111
V	4	1111
X		
Y		
Z	2	11

ABOVE: Frequency tables, which are the
foundation of the science of cryptanalysis.

by an infantry officer, Captain Parker Hitt, who had written a *Manual for the Solution of Military Ciphers* for a course at the U.S. Signal Corps School, Fort Leavenworth, Kansas. This slim volume, of just 100 pages, remains one of the great unclassified signals intelligence classics. Hitt outlined the two basic methods of encipherment – transposition and substitution – and described how ciphers could be solved by the construction of alphabetic frequency tables. This was the system that had been developed in the Admiralty's Room 40 and was founded on the belief that in any text of a particular language certain letters will appear in a reasonably predictable ratio to other letters. Once this principle has been grasped, Hitt asserted, "no message should be considered indecipherable". Of interception, Hitt observed, "All radio messages sent out can be copied at hostile stations within radio range. If the enemy can get a fine wire within one hundred feet of a buzzer line or within thirty feet of a telegraph line, the message can be copied by induction." Hitt also gave some excellent advice for future signals intelligence analysts:

> The preamble, "place from", date, address and signature give most important clues as to the language of the cipher, the cipher method probably used, and even the subject matter of the message. If the whole of a telegraphic or radio message is in cipher, it is highly probable that the preamble, "place from" etc. are in an operator's cipher and are distinct from the body of the message. As these operator's ciphers are necessarily simple, an attempt should always be made to discover, by means of analysis to be set forth later, the exact extent of the operator's cipher and then to decipher the parts of the message enciphered with it.

Using Hitt's *Manual* as a guide, Yardley had begun examining the messages that passed through his hands. On one occasion, he overheard a cable office in New York informing the White House operator that a telegram of 500 coded groups was about to be transmitted from Colonel House to President Woodrow Wilson. Yardley copied the telegram and solved the message within two hours. This achievement led Yardley to write a lengthy *Exposition on the Solution of American Diplomatic Codes*, which caused the State Department to introduce a new code, but Yardley broke that too.

Although the British had gone to some lengths to conceal Room 40's activities, the State Department was aware that "England maintains a large bureau for solving diplomatic correspondence" and assumed that U.S. cables were routinely intercepted. Like the Germans, the Americans had complete faith in the integrity of their cipher arrangements, or at least until Yardley demonstrated his prowess. For the first time the State Department acknowledged that its most sensitive communications had probably been read by the British; its response was to appoint Yardley to the secret unit which subsequently became the War Department Cipher Bureau. By 1918, Yardley employed a staff of 150 and enjoyed an annual budget of $100,000.

Ironically, as soon as the U.S. entered the war, the British government informed President Wilson that it considered the War Department's method of coding cable grams entirely unsafe and "a serious menace to secrecy". The news was also conveyed that the Germans were probably intercepting all of America's cable traffic. There is no evidence to support that claim, but no doubt the British Admiralty was anxious to persuade its new allies to exercise caution. Washington was spun a yarn that enemy submarines often tapped underwater cables. Apparently by "stretching other wires alongside for a distance of several hundred feet telegraph operators stationed in the submarines can copy the passing messages by induction". Yardley seems to have accepted this, for both the State and War Departments quickly altered their coding practices and became more security conscious.

09. COMPTON MACKENZIE

THE FIRST INSIDER DISCLOSURES

THE QUINTESSENTIAL SCOT

In October 1932 Compton Mackenzie attempted to publish the third volume of his war memoirs, entitled *Greek Memories*, in which he gave a detailed account of his work for MI6 in the Aegean in 1917. Not only did Mackenzie reveal that Mansfield Smith-Cumming was known within Whitehall by the initial "C", but he identified dozens of officers with whom he had served during the war, including a few that had remained active in the region after the conclusion of hostilities. Mackenzie's book, which had been preceded by *Extremes Meet* – in which he had described his experiences in fictional terms, without experiencing any difficulties – was instantly the subject of a ban and a short time later the author appeared at the Old Bailey charged with breaching the Official Secrets Act. What made the prosecution's case so awkward was the fact that Mackenzie had received an informal consent to publish from Sir Eric Holt-Wilson, one of his former colleagues in the Near East, who had subsequently been appointed deputy director-general of the Security Service. Holt-Wilson, whose name appeared in the text, sat in the well of the court during the proceedings and saw Mackenzie plead guilty and be fined £100.

Mackenzie was deeply resentful of his treatment and, to pay the costs of his defence, later wrote the hugely popular *Water on the Brain* as a wickedly entertaining satire on the Secret Service. It was not until 1938 that a sanitized version of *Greek Memories* was published, with MI6's permission. The first volume of his war memoirs, *Gallipoli Memories*, was published without challenge and the sequel to *Greek Memories*, *First Athenian Memories*, was released

ABOVE: Compton Mackenzie as a Royal Marines officer before he was transferred in 1916 to MI6 in the Aegean.

in March 1931. The fourth, *Aegean Memories*, was published in 1940 and dedicated to brother officer and lifelong friend, Edward Knoblock. More than 50 years after the trial, University Publications of America acquired a rare copy of the first, unexpurgated, edition and released it with the offending passages highlighted in bold print.

Mackenzie had joined MI6 in 1916 at the age of 33, after he had been invalided out of the Royal Marines, having been wounded in the

ABOVE: SS *Politician*, the cargo ship that foundered off Eriskay in March 1941, later the basis of Compton Mackenzie's novel *Whisky Galore*.

RIGHT: Mackenzie, who founded the Scottish Nationalist Party, loved the Highlands and Scottish life in the Islands, but actually had been born in West Hartlepool.

Dardanelles offensive. He was by then already a successful author, having made his name with *Sinister Street*. Born in West Hartlepool, he had read modern history at Magdalen College, Oxford, and had joined the 1st Hertfordshire Regiment in 1900.

Among his many later literary successes were *Extraordinary Women* and the comedy *Whisky Galore*, which was based upon the true story of the wreck of a freighter, the SS *Politician*, loaded with a cargo of export whisky during the Second World War. After the Second World War, which Mackenzie spent on the island of Barra, he helped one of his former subordinates, Wilfred Macartney, to publish the story of Eddie Chapman, the MI5 double agent codenamed ZIGZAG, but the enterprise failed.

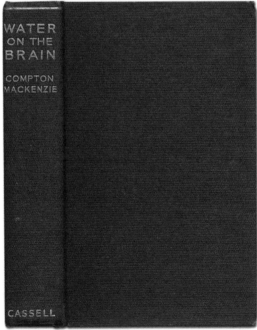

Macartney had been convicted of espionage on behalf of the Soviets in 1928 but this misfortune had not prevented Mackenzie from giving him his support when he attempted to publicize Chapman's remarkable story. He was always willing to back unpopular causes – he was one of the few to publicly support P.G. Wodehouse when the latter was in danger of being prosecuted for his unwise broadcasts for the Nazis.

Mackenzie died in Edinburgh in November 1972, 20 years after he had received his knighthood, having published his tenth volume of autobiography.

LEFT: Mackenzie published his satire *Water on the Brain* in retaliation for his prosecution under the Official Secrets Act in October 1932.

ABOVE: Magdalen College, Oxford, where Mackenzie graduated in 1904 with a degree in modern history.

OPPOSITE: Mackenzie's romanticised story of the salvage by Hebridean islanders of the *Politician*'s cargo of whisky became a movie in 1949.

10. LIEUTENANT WILFRED MACARTNEY

A SPY UNCOVERED IN LONDON REVEALED

AN INTERNATIONAL SOVIET SPY-RING

THE TURNCOAT

The son of a wealthy engineer who was the proprietor of Malta's electric tram system, Wilfred Macartney first came to the attention of the police in February 1926 when he had been sentenced to nine months for smashing a jeweller's shop window in Albemarle Street.

In 1915, at the age of only 16, Macartney failed an army medical because of poor eyesight, but managed to join the Royal Army Medical Corps 3rd Field Ambulance as a driver and was sent to France, where he secured a commission in the Royal Scots. After some months his eyes deteriorated and he was forced to resign his commission.

After treatment, he was recommissioned in the Essex Regiment, then stationed in Malta. From there he went to Egypt, where he was taken on by the Staff as a censor. His first posting was to the Aegean, under the command of Captain Compton Mackenzie, the Royal Marines officer who headed British intelligence operations in the eastern Mediterranean theatre. Macartney worked directly for Mackenzie in the cover of a port control officer until September 1917 when he returned to France with the 52nd Division. In September the following year he was taken prisoner at Cambrai but made a daring escape from the Germans by jumping out of a train near Aix-la-Chapelle. This achievement was rewarded with a Certificate of Merit from the Army Council. After the Armistice, Macartney, now aged 19, was attached to the Berlin–Baghdad Railway Mission in Constantinople, as railway transport officer. He left the army as a lieutenant in 1919.

ABOVE: Chapman's astonishing bravery as the double agent ZIGZAG prompted his MI5 case officer, Michael Ryde, to give evidence for him during his postwar trial.

Macartney was a contributor to the *Sunday Worker* newspaper. After his release from prison in October 1926 he wrote an article entitled "Boss Propaganda in the Scrubs" and three weeks later

"The Fate of the Good Union Men" in the same paper. His criminal record also shows two fines for being drunk and disorderly in the West End in January and February 1927.

In March 1927 a Lloyds insurance underwriter, George Monckland, approached Admiral Sir Reginald Hall to seek advice about a request he had received from Macartney about any information relating to the export of weapons to Finland. Apparently Macartney had shown him a typewritten letter and questionnaire dated 22 March from a "K. J. Johnson", supposedly the Soviet master-spy in London. Macartney had explained that this was the name used by whoever was directing Soviet operations in Britain.

Informed by Hall, MI5 was determined to identify the whole network and arranged an elaborate deception for Macartney by providing him with a genuine secret document and keeping him under surveillance. A Royal Air Force (RAF) handbook marked "secret" and entitled *Regulations for Training the Flying Personnel of the Royal Air Force* was given to Monckland to give to Macartney for onward transmission to the Russians, the Air Ministry having assured MI5 that the document was obsolete and about to be replaced by an up-to-date issue. Special Branch was mobilized to follow Macartney after he had left Monckland's flat in Hertford Street, Mayfair, and he was observed to pass the RAF manual to a Russian who was known to be a member of the Soviet trade delegation. Accordingly, on 12 May a mass of policemen congregated outside ARCOS House, the offices the trade delegation shared with the All-Russian Co-Operative Society (ARCOS). It was a raiding party that consisted of about 100 uniformed City of London policemen, 50 Special Branch officers and a small contingent of Foreign Office interpreters who were to translate the documents seized.

The raid eventually came to an end at midnight on 16 May 1927, after just over 103 hours and several protests from the Soviets. Macartney had made a panic-stricken telephone call to Monckland soon after the raid had started, telling him to destroy any incriminating papers he might have collected. The RAF handbook was never found but the regular Soviet courier between Chesham House and Moorgate, Robert Koling, had been searched and several compromising letters relating to future trade union plans in the United Kingdom were recovered. Additionally, the trade delegation cipher clerk, Anton Miller, was caught carrying a list of Communist International (Comintern) cover addresses in Canada, Argentina, Colombia, Guatemala, Uruguay, Mexico, Brazil, Chile, South Africa, Australia and the United States.

On 26 May the government published a White Paper to announce that diplomatic relations with Moscow, which had been originally initiated by Ramsay MacDonald in 1921, would be severed forthwith. Evidence of the Soviet Union's attempts at subversion were included in the two-part document. The first reproduced various incriminating letters found during the ARCOS raid; the second dealt with decrypted telegrams intercepted by the Foreign Office. MI5 passed on copies of these to other European counter-intelligence agencies, who made their own raids on local ARCOS branches.

After his hasty telephone call to Monckland, Macartney recovered himself and was soon in contact again, in spite of a slight brush with the law caused by another drinking session. MI5 intervened behind the scenes and all charges against Macartney for this were quietly dropped to prevent his being sent to prison, an event MI5 wished to avoid. For the next six months Monckland tried to extract more information from Macartney about the network, and Special Branch followed him on his travels, which included a trip to Berlin.

During the early part of August 1927 Macartney made a couple of visits to a secretarial firm in the Edgware Road and had several letters and reports typed up, apparently for the elusive "Mr Johnson". Each time he went to the typists Special Branch

detectives called in shortly afterwards and took away the dictation notes. Gradually, the evidence mounted that a spy-ring really did exist. A copy of one report for the spy-master recorded "expenses paid", and "Davis" and "Barton" were mentioned as having received sums from Macartney. It seemed likely that Davis was a sergeant in the Tank Corps and had provided Macartney with some basic intelligence about British mechanized armour during a visit to Aldershot and on a later trip to Tidworth, timed to coincide with military exercises.

Macartney managed to obtain a false passport in the name of William Frank Hudson and he once boasted to Monckland that he had access to genuine passports, issued by the Passport Office in Petty France but without any record remaining at the offices. MI5 immediately contacted the Passport Office and received confirmation of his claim. A valid passport had been issued to a William Frank Hudson but mysteriously there was no copy of the original application.

By November 1927 Macartney had arranged for Monckland to exchange letters with "Mr Johnson" and a meeting was set up for the afternoon of 16 November 1927 in the Marble Arch Cinema Café. Monckland was to sit alone at a table reading a book and "Mr Johnson" would come over and introduce himself. Monckland complied with the instructions and sat down to read a copy of *The Spy* by Upton Sinclair. He was soon approached by a young foreigner in his early twenties who announced himself as "Mr Johnson" and enquired about shipments of arms to the Baltic states and the quality of information Monckland might be able to provide. After a brief conversation Monckland agreed to a second rendezvous the following day

LEFT: City of London Police guard the premises of Arcos Ltd as the offices are searched by MI5 for a classified RAF handbook.

when, he claimed, he would provide "Mr Johnson" with some examples of the intelligence to which he had access. The meeting would also be attended by Macartney.

The following day "Mr Johnson" was arrested while he waited for his two companions. Macartney was intercepted at Hampstead tube station, right across the road from the agreed meeting place. Both men were taken to Scotland Yard where they were interrogated and "Mr Johnson" was found to be Georg Hansen, a 24-year-old German student who had registered as an alien at Bow Street in July 1927. Both men were charged with offences under the Official Secrets Act and tried at the Old Bailey in January the following year. Both men received sentences of 10 years, to be served concurrently with a further sentence of two years' hard labour.

ABOVE: Wilfred Macartney and Eddie Chapman at their trial in March 1946 for breaches of the Official Secrets Act.

OPPOSITE: George Monckland, the Lloyd's underwriter who reported the suspicious interest paid by Wilfred Macartney in shipments of arms to Finland.

Upon his release Macartney published *Walls Have Mouths* in 1936 and *Zigzag* in 1937, and volunteered for the International Brigade to fight during the Spanish Civil War. He became commandant of the British battalion and was wounded in January 1937.

In March 1946 Macartney was prosecuted a second time, for collaborating with Eddie Chapman to publish his story as a wartime MI5 double agent. On that occasion he escaped with a fine, but in 1950 he was declared bankrupt. He died in December 1970.

ARCOS

The ARCOS building itself had cost over £300,000 and included concrete-lined vaults which were off-limits to anyone other than the most senior of the Russian staff. The trade delegation, under the chairmanship of Mr L. Khinchuk, employed a staff of over 400, 233 of whom were Russians but the delegation paid the wages of only 35, the rest being "attached" to the All-Russian Co-Operative Society. The intercepts broken by the Foreign Office had long ago proved the diplomatic mission, the trade delegation and ARCOS to be involved in subversive activities in Britain. Accordingly, the Secretary of State for War went to Sir William Joynson-Hicks, the Home Secretary, on the evening of 11 May 1927 and explained how MI5 was sure the Russians were in possession of a secret RAF document. He proposed the massive police raid on the Russian trade delegation with a warrant issued by a magistrate under the Official Secrets Act. The Home Secretary agreed, but only after he had been reassured on a few important points and after consultations with the prime minister, Stanley Baldwin, and the Foreign Secretary, Sir Austen Chamberlain. These issues included the diplomatic immunity enjoyed by Khinchuk and his Soviet staff. Sir Wyndham Childs, the head of Special Branch, explained how the police could exploit a loophole overlooked by the Russians. While the delegation certainly had immunity from search, their shared offices with ARCOS Ltd, a company registered in Britain with limited liability, did not. As there was no physical division between the two Russian offices, when the trade delegation chairman made his protest about an illegal search, as he surely would, the police could reply that they had only entered the premises of ARCOS. The Home Secretary was impressed, and the warrant was issued.

11. JESSIE JORDAN

THE ORIGINS OF FBI COUNTER-INTELLIGENCE

THE DUNDEE MAIL DROP

In the inter-war period MI5 identified 30 German agents or persons at whom the Germans had made a pitch. Twenty-one were British, many of whom made no attempt to collect intelligence of value to the Germans but simply passed on items of little significance in a bid to get maximum reward for minimum effort. They had received no training at all, and the Abwehr's methods appeared inept. Half of the cases involved individuals who were never in a position to procure intelligence of any value. Among the more suitable people whom the Germans recruited or attempted to recruit were four ex-officers, four businessmen and four members of the armed forces; most of them reported the approach to the authorities immediately.

The Germans recruited by responding to small ads in the newspapers, especially those from ex-officers, businessmen and specialists with a technical knowledge seeking jobs. The Germans also placed advertisements themselves in British papers, offering jobs for commercial and technical experts. From 1936 the Hamburg Abwehrstelle (Abwehr station) stepped up its efforts, so that 26 of the 30 known cases came to MI5's notice between 1936 and the outbreak of war. Of these, three were cases where the Germans recruited them so that their addresses (one in England, one in Scotland and one in Ireland) could be used by the Hamburg Abwehrstelle as mail-drops where it received messages from agents in the U.S. and France.

Eleven of the 30 agents told MI5 about the German approach; nine were exposed by mail intercepts, five were denounced by private individuals whose suspicions had been aroused, one was reported

ABOVE: The official seal of the FBI.

by an immigration officer, and one was denounced by an anonymous informant; the other two were uncovered by accident. Of the 11 agents who reported they had been recruited by the Germans (who would probably have escaped detection) six were recruited via a personal contact.

Three Post Office boxes, registered in the names of different women, yielded a great deal of information. Mrs Duncombe in London received intelligence collected in France, while Mrs Jessie Jordan, a 51-year-old hairdresser of Kinloch Street, Dundee, acted as an intermediary for an important spy based in the United States.

The widow of a German soldier killed during the Great War, Jordan had spent most of her adult life in Germany and had returned to Dundee to open a small business. At the age of 16 she had ran away from her mother (she never knew her father) and

ABOVE: Mrs Jessie Jordan's daughter Marga and her husband in May 1939 after her mother's trial in Edinburgh.

found a job as a domestic servant. Four years later she met a German named Jordan in Scotland and returned with him to Germany, where they were wed. After the war she had married again but had subsequently obtained a divorce from her second husband. Eventually, she had returned to Scotland, partly in disgust at the anti-Semitic behaviour she had witnessed. Although she was not herself a Jew, the name Jordan, a name she had readopted after the failure of her second marriage, had Jewish significance. At the end of 1937 her postman asked whether he could keep the stamps from her overseas mail as she was receiving letters from all over the world and he was keen to build up his collection. Mrs Jordan refused in such strong terms that the postman reported the matter to his supervisor, and the Post Office soon established that not only was the hairdresser getting an unusual amount of mail, but she was posting a great deal too. The bulk of her post went to America but she also received letters from Holland, France, Germany, Sweden and South America.

ABOVE: Rumrich, Voss and Glaser leave the court in New York handcuffed after their indictment on espionage charges.

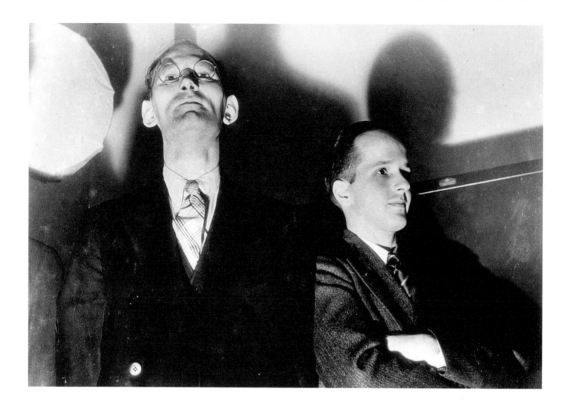

ABOVE: The German spies Otto Voss and Gunther Rumrich were arrested by the FBI in New York, having been compromised by Mrs Jordan's mail-drop.

Based on a tip from the Dundee City Police, MI5 intercepted Jordan's mail and learned that she was acting as a postbox for the Abwehrstelle. At the end of January 1937, the deputy director of MI5's B Division, Guy Liddell, went to Washington, DC, and explained to the director of the FBI, J. Edgar Hoover, that Mrs Jordan had been in communication with a "Mr Kron" in New York. Hoover checked the address and established that "Herr Kron" was Günther Rumrich, a Sudeten German who had become a naturalized American. His record showed that he had served seven years in the army and had been sentenced for desertion and embezzlement of mess funds from Fort Missoula in Montana. The FBI kept Rumrich under surveillance so the Jordan postbox could be monitored, but on 16 February 1937 he was arrested by detectives from the Aliens Squad.

Just as the FBI were being told about MI5's suspicions concerning Rumrich, the State Department's New York Passport Office had asked the Aliens Squad to investigate a phoney request for 50 blank passports, which were to be delivered to the Taft Hotel. Apparently Rumrich had been instructed by Karl Schleuter, a steward on the SS *Europa*, to obtain 50 passports for the Abwehrstelle. Rumrich had tried to do this by impersonating a senior State Department official, Edward Weston, an Under-Secretary of State.

After his arrest Rumrich confessed that, having read Colonel Walter Nicolai's memoirs, he had written to the Berlin *Völkischer Beobachter*, the major Nazi daily, offering his services. He asked that if the Germans were interested in the information that "a high official in the United States Army" could pass they should place an advertisement in the *New York Times*. It was to read: "Theodor

Koerner – Letter received" and give an address where he could contact the Abwehrstelle. In the event the Abwehrstelle had instructed him to reply to "Sanders, Postbox 629, Hamburg 1, Germany". The announcement had duly appeared on 6 April 1936 and "Herr Kron" and Rumrich went into action. He operated for 20 months between May 1936 and February 1938 and succeeded in passing a considerable amount of intelligence to Hamburg via Dundee.

Under interrogation Rumrich revealed that apart from Mrs Jordan his contact with the Abwehrstelle had been via Karl Schleuter and his girlfriend, Johanna Hoffmann, an American from Queens who was working on the *Europa* as a hairdresser. With the arrest of Johanna Hoffmann, the FBI was able to eliminate a major German network in America.

Others implicated in the spy-ring were William Lonkowski, an aircraft mechanic from Silesia who had worked in various American aircraft factories until an incident with U.S. Customs in September 1935, Werner Gudenberg, a young engineering draughtsman, and Otto Voss, who worked for the Sikorsky factory at Farmingdale, Long Island. In turn Dr Ignatz Giebl, a Great War artillery officer and graduate of medicine at Fordham University, was implicated in the Nazi conspiracy. A Grand Jury investigation was started and the Abwehrstelle officer at the centre of the operation, Erich Phieffer (alias "N. Spielman", "Dr Erdhoff" and merely "Herr Doktor") was identified as the major conspirator, based at Wilhelmshaven.

Mrs Jordan was arrested on 2 March 1938 and, when her house was searched, the police found a rather amateurish sketch map of Fife and a list of coastguard stations between Montrose and Kirkcaldy. Jordan admitted her espionage and confirmed she had received various small sums for her service to the Abwehrstelle. Accordingly, on 15 May 1938 she was sentenced to four years' imprisonment. Jordan served her sentence at Perth prison.

When Rumrich's brother was arrested in Prague he was found to be in possession of the address of a Mrs Gertrude Brandy in Dublin – this was the third mail-drop. Clandestine examination of her correspondence showed that she was receiving accurate and therefore dangerous intelligence messages from a French merchant navy officer, Ensign Marc Aubert, who was arrested at the end of 1938 and shot in January 1939. When news of the execution reached Ireland, Mrs Brandy fled to Germany, unhindered by the Irish intelligence service, the G-2, which had kept her under surveillance at MI5's request.

ABOVE: Johanna Hoffman, the SS *Europa* hairdresser who acted as a transatlantic courier for the Abwehr.

PART 3

THE SECOND WORLD WAR

12. OPERATION CANNED GOODS

THE FALSE FLAG OPERATION AT GLEIWITZ

THAT TRIGGERED THE SECOND WORLD WAR

STARTING A WORLD WAR

In August 1939, the Nazi government in Germany was preparing for an attack on Poland, an event that would trigger the Second World War. In preparation, the Nazi Party intelligence agency Sicherheitsdienst (SD) was given the task of providing the pretext for the imminent offensive.

The SD's more conventional counterpart, the Abwehr, collected military intelligence through a fragmented regional network of offices based at the Wehrmacht's headquarters in each of Germany's military districts. Meanwhile, the SD was a centralized unit controlled by the Nazi Party, staffed by zealots of the party's military branch, the SS, and dedicated to the acquisition and analysis of political intelligence. Founded in 1932 and directed by Reinhard Heydrich, the SD operated in parallel with the more overt party police, the Gestapo, and

ABOVE: Alfred Naujocks, of the Sicherheitsdienst (the SS intelligence agency), who fired the first shots of the conflict.

ABOVE: A British newspaper report of 1 September 1939 on the outbreak of hostilities.

ABOVE: Reich Propaganda Ministry personnel accompany a group of foreign journalists to the site of an alleged atrocity supposedly committed against German-speaking Poles.

developed experience of subversion and sabotage, first in Hitler's Anschluss campaign to absorb Austria, and then by acting as a catalyst for the Sudetenland crisis in Czechoslovakia.

In both examples the SD devised and ran classic "black operations" by distributing propaganda, spreading false rumours, stage-managing demonstrations and by the intimidation or outright elimination of political opponents. Through the skilful manipulation of the media, and by employing ruthless covert tactics against adversaries, the SD took insidious control over the political climate. This brought about the circumstances in which the Reich's policy of expansion could be fulfilled without the need for a prolonged military engagement,

which would risk organized resistance and international condemnation. In this way, the SD's innovative model avoided the necessity for direct, overt cross-border intervention or annexation until the last moment. Then, in a swift coup-de-main, order would be restored following a period of apparent, but actually largely synthetically orchestrated, chaos.

The SD's clandestine role in pursuing the Nazi Party's objectives gave the organization a unique status in Berlin, where it protected its interests by maintaining surveillance on potential enemies, and compromising others through the discreet management of a notorious bordello, the Salon Kitty. This establishment, ostensibly run by the accommodating Kitty Schmidt, was popular with foreign visitors and diplomats, as well as influential politicians, and it provided Heydrich with

ABOVE: A propaganda photo intended to illustrate total support from the local German-speaking population in Poland for the Nazi invasion.

OPPOSITE: The radio mast at Gleiwitz, scene of the SD's most notorious false-flag operation.

unprecedented leverage in the German capital. The full extent of the SD's activities only became known after the war when a senior SD officer, Walter Schellenberg, was brought to London to undergo prolonged interrogation by MI5. General Schellenberg's hair-raising account of the SD's grasp on power within the Nazi structure provided an unprecedented insight into how Heydrich and his subordinates were assigned the most sensitive and politically explosive tasks, including the incident that served to spark off global hostilities.

Codenamed CANNED GOODS, the scheme was based on a previous operation conducted by the SD in January 1935 when an attack had been made on an anti-Nazi radio station in the Czech village of Slapy, a fabricated incident intended to raise tensions on the Sudeten frontier. On that occasion the short-wave station's engineer, Rudolf Formis, had been murdered by an SD officer, Alfred Naujocks. Naujocks was now given the new mission to Gleiwitz by his chief, Reinhard Heydrich. His objective was to create a narrative of alleged provocations, supposedly a series of incursions across the Polish–German border into German territory. On the night of 31 August 1939, Naujocks took control of the medium-wave radio station with its iconic tower – at 120 metres (400 feet), Europe's highest wooden structure – and broadcast a short anti-Nazi message in Polish before planting a bullet-ridden dead body in the studio. More corpses, actually those of prisoners from the Dachau concentration camp, were dressed in Polish uniforms and positioned on the station's perimeter for the benefit of the press, selected representatives of which were invited to take photographs of the staged scene, thereby providing the proof required by Berlin. This wholly fabricated episode was cited by the German government as the reason for launching a major offensive that in three short weeks led to the occupation of Warsaw.

Naujocks, originally from Kiel, had joined the SD as a driver, but had been swiftly promoted and was enthusiastic about his distasteful assignments. He would later participate in the abduction at Venlo of two MI6 officers (see pages 70–75) and played a controversial role in the suppression of the resistance in Denmark. In November 1944 he was detained by the U.S. Army when he disclosed his version of the Gleiwitz incident. He escaped custody before he could face prosecution for war crimes and, although a fugitive, lived quite openly in Hamburg until his death in April 1966 at the age of 54, having collaborated with Günter Peis to publish his memoirs, *The Man who Started the War*.

Walter Schellenberg, who gave evidence at Nuremberg against his former SD rival Ernst Kaltenbrunner, also escaped any significant punishment for his involvement in SD atrocities. Despite receiving a six-year prison sentence in 1949, he was released in December 1950 and moved to Switzerland and then to Italy, where he died in March 1952.

13. THE VENLO INCIDENT

A COUNTER-INTELLIGENCE OPERATION THAT LED TO THE ABDUCTION OF TWO BRITISH INTELLIGENCE AGENTS AND BROUGHT ABOUT THE COLLAPSE OF THE Z SPY ORGANIZATION

BORDER ABDUCTION

On Monday, 4 September 1939, the first day of the Second World War, Major Richard Stevens, the MI6 station commander in The Hague received unexpected instructions from London to cooperate with Captain Sigismund Payne Best, a somewhat larger-than-life English businessman resident in The Hague and prominent member of the local expatriate community. Best, then aged 55, was not particularly well regarded, partly because of his "more English than the English" postures, and partly because of his ostentatious manner, habitually wearing spats and sporting a monocle. Although he was less than popular, his Dutch wife Maria Margareta was a renowned hostess and was well connected in Holland through her father, Admiral van Rees. Best had also been decorated with the OBE, as well as a French Legion d'honneur and a Belgian Croix de Guerre, and he was The Hague's resident Z officer, representing MI6's Z organization. This was a parallel network of British businessmen and journalists who had been recruited by Claude Dansey, formerly the Rome station commander, with the intention of working independently of the local PCO. The British Passport Control Office was well-known to be a convenient cover for intelligence personnel but the Z network, operating under various commercial guises, was rather less transparent and allowed its members to travel across Europe freely, on apparently legitimate business, without attracting suspicion.

ABOVE: Richard Stevens, the MI6 station commander in The Hague and the local Z organization representative, Sigismund Payne Best, photographed by the SD after they had been seized at the Café Backus.

Over the past several months Best had been cultivating what he believed to be a ring of anti-Nazis in Germany via several refugees who had managed to make their way to Holland. His link to the mainly Catholic refugees was his Dutch aide, Peter Vrooburgh, who in turn had a useful German source named Dr Franz Fischer, formerly a major coal distributor in Württemberg, and rated by both Best and Dansey as an important sub-agent. Fischer had many useful connections, especially in Munich where his brother was a well-known theatrical director.

Best's dilemma, about which he consulted the PCO, concerned a request made by Fischer through Vrooburgh. Apparently Fischer claimed to possess some momentous intelligence and would only impart it if he was able to make direct contact with

DAILY MIRROR, Thursday, Nov. 23, 1939.

Daily Mirror

No. 11,221 ✦ ✦ ✦ ONE PENNY
Registered at the G.P.O. as a Newspaper.

NAZIS MURDER BRITISH AGENT

—Amsterdam Report

CAPTAIN STEVENS, an official of the British Passport Control office at The Hague, who with Mr. Best, a brother official, was kidnapped over the Dutch border at Venlo by Nazi S.S. troops, has been murdered, according to a report reaching Amsterdam.

Information from Germany states that Captain Stevens and Mr. Best resisted their kidnappers and were beaten unmercifully in the car, which was racing to the Nazi Customs House close at hand.

Both Britons were lifted unconscious from the car at the guard-house, but Captain Stevens never rallied. The report adds that he died next day from his injuries.

Mr. Best is still receiving hospital treatment.

Hardly an hour passes in Berlin without the publication of new "sensational particulars" about the arrested German Georg Elser, who is alleged to have confessed that he placed the bomb from which Hitler narrowly escaped at Munich, and that he had been the tool of the leader of the Anti-Nazi Black Front, Dr. Otto Strasser, and of the British Secret Service.

Obviously the Nazis are using the Reichstag fire scheme of manufacturing new details every day.

Himmler Knew It Before

But Dr. Strasser yesterday gave the lie to the Gestapo.

"The Nazi public is learning now that I have organised the Munich bomb plot," he told journalists, who saw him in his secret hiding place in Paris. "But Herr Himmler, chief of the Gestapo, knew it before.

"For he demanded my extradition from the Swiss authorities on the morning after the bombing, alleging that I was responsible

"I had just four hours to leave Switzerland and to escape to France.

"The whole story was prepared beforehand and the 'revelations' of Elser, another van Lubbe the scapegoat of the Reichstag fire) were carefully prepared before the bomb exploded

"Did Not Know Bomb Setter"

"I don't know Elser, and, moreover, I am certain he is not one of my men," continued Dr. Strasser, "I have never known the Mr. Best or Captain Stevens, mentioned by Himmler.

"If the Gestapo decided that it would be useful to launch an accusation against our 'Black Front,' that convinces me of the power of our organisation.

"But we have nothing to fear. They try to strike the 'Black Front,' which possesses men the Gestapo will never discover, working not only within each Nazi party organisation but within the Gestapo itself.

"The Gestapo tried frequently to assassinate or abduct me. The last attempt on my life failed through the devotion of my friends in the Gestapo."

NAZI SHIP DISGUISE FOILED

A BRITISH warship intercepted a German ship, Bertha Fisser (4,110 tons) yesterday, as she was making a dash for Iceland from Bergen, Norway, masquerading under other names.

Her crew tried to scuttle her, but failed. They took to the boats too quickly, and the ship ran on the rocks

An examination of her wreckage made it clear that she had been masquerading under the names of Emden I and Ada.

The German crew was picked up by the British warship

Bid to Beach Ship

Tugs were last night towing the Italian steamer Fianona (6,660 tons), badly holed by a mine off the south-east coast, in the hope of beaching her

A lifeboat was hurriedly launched when the noise of the explosion was heard. Many people asleep on shore were awakened by the concussion.

Fortunately for the ship she was light. This made her more buoyant, but she took in so much water that her crew had to keep at the pumps all night

After the lifeboat had stood by the Fianona all night she was called to two steamers which had been in collision

When the Norwegian steamer Brarena (6,996 tons) of Oslo was in a broadside collision with the Greek steamer Nicolaos Piangos (4,499 tons) the force of the collision was so great, that the Nicolaos Piangos suffered serious damage amidships besides having her boats smashed

The Brarena received serious damage to her bows

Paralysed by Baling

How two men stood with their feet over a hole in their boat throughout the night and another had his right arm paralysed through baling out water was told yesterday when the crew of thirteen of the Fleetwood trawler Delphine arrived at a Northern Ireland town.

The Delphine was sunk off the north-west coast of Ireland by the same U-Boat which sank the Thomas Hankins, also a Fleetwood trawler.

The crew, who left for Fleetwood, were all uninjured except the mate, Ronald Heather, of Fleetwood, whose arm was paralysed. He had been baling water out all night from the ship's boat.

It was stormy, and when their boat was taking off it was damaged against the side of the trawler

RALPH RICHARDSON IN PLANE RESCUE

Hero of many spectacular flying escapades of the films Sub-Lieutenant Ralph Richardson, R.N.V.R., shaken and bruised after his plane made a forced landing in Hampshire yesterday, helped to rescue his wireless operator from the machine.

The star of "The Lion Has Wings," the film which shows the Kiel Canal raid, got into difficulties, his machine losing height and panc:.ng into a garden.

Richardson jumped out and helped to rescue Able-Seaman Alan Todd, who sprained his right arm.

Mr. William Compton, aged seventy-eight, was in his garden, and the port wing flashed just over his head.

In "Q Planes," a flying film, Ralph Richardson played the part of a British secret agent. He owns his own aeroplane.

Miss Fiona Tatchell, daughter of a London specialist, after her wedding to the Hon. James Craig, son of Viscount Craigavon, Prime Minister of Northern Ireland, at St. Columba's, Pont-street (London), yesterday.

DUTCH BAN SAILINGS

HITLER will not be able to send any more of his goods on Dutch ships.

For yesterday, on the advice of the Netherland. Government, Dutch shipowners cancelled all sailings from their ports

No explanation was given, but the step followed the British announcement that German export cargoes on neutral vessels would be subject to seizure.

Shipowners held a meeting to consider the dangers to shipping including the peril of mines

Ten Million Tons

The Amerika liner Rotterdam left Rotterdam yesterday for New York before the ban was enforced. Doubt was expressed that the liner Statendam would return from the United States until the situation has been clarified.

Ten million tons of German exports were transhipped from Rotterdam and Amsterdam in the first nine months of this year.

₊ Berlin threatens as Britain acts: Page 2.

ITALIAN KING OF HUNGARY?

The Rome correspondent of the Danish newspaper Politiken says there are persistent rumours that a member of the House of Savoy —the Italian Royal House—may occupy the throne of Hungary.

It has even been stated that King Victor Emmanuel may be given the title of King of Hungary, and that Admiral Horthy, the present Regent, may become his Viceroy. Italy and Hungary, according to the report, would remain independent of each other.—Exchange.

DUCHY PAINTS FRONTIERS

Luxembourg is to mark its borders with blocks of white cement and luminous signs for the benefit of belligerent aircraft.

NAZI RAIDERS 'CALL' AGAIN

SIX Nazi raiders flew over the Shetlands yesterday and dropped bombs, which did no damage They were driven off by anti-aircraft guns.

The machines circled several times, flying very low, and tracer bullets were fired at them.

In one town an air raid warning was given. Fifteen minutes later the "All clear" sounded. South-East England had its usual daily raid yesterday

A single machine flew over the Thames Estuary, escaped a barrage by anti-aircraft guns, then sped over South Essex. No air raid warning was given, and crowds who watched in the streets saw no fighters go up.

When British pursuit planes made their appearance, the raider swept down, dodged through the countryside by hedge-hopping tactics.

Searchlight posts fired their machine-guns at it.

But the lone raider—' big machine—apparently escaped

"Diving, Twisting"

An eye-witness who said the plane went right over his garage, added: "Our fighters were diving, criss-crossing, firing at it from above and below, and all the time the German plane was trying all kinds of manœuvres to shake them off.

"They were still firing at it when it went out of sight. It seemed no higher than the telegraph poles."

In a third raid yesterday a twin-engined black plane flew over the East Coast. An anti-aircraft battery fired at it and it turned out to sea.

Afterwards, British pursuit planes flew in the same direction.

It was officially revealed yesterday that one of the raiders the night before—a seaplane—dived low to machine-gun coast defences and was answered with fire from the ground. The machine climbed into mist and cloud and disappeared.

The Nazis admitted yesterday that one of Tuesday's reconnaissance planes did not return. This machine was brought down by fighters at sea.

Black-Out Walkers, Keep to the Left

Here's some black-out advice for pedestrians from Captain Wallace, Minister of Transport:—

Walk on the left hand side of the pavement. But in a one-way street don't walk near the kerb in the same direction as the traffic.

By remembering these points much danger and confusion will be eliminated.

ABOVE: *The Daily Mirror* in the UK incorrectly reports the death of Major Stevens.

an official from the British Secret Service. After some discussion, Stevens agreed to seek advice from Dansey and MI6 headquarters, but Dansey was uncontactable in Switzerland and the rest of the organization was mildly dysfunctional following the recent death of the chief, Admiral Hugh Sinclair. Accordingly the acting chief, Stewart Menzies, gave his consent to Stevens's plan.

At a preliminary meeting Best had been introduced to a Major Solms, a Luftwaffe officer who demanded confirmation that Best was indeed acting with the full authority of MI6. His credentials had been established to the satisfaction of Solms when Best had arranged for a particular item to be inserted into the BBC's German News Service, twice, on 11 October 1939. This was to be just one of several meetings that Best unwittingly attended with representatives of the Nazi intelligence service (SD). They played a tantalizingly elaborate game, which resulted in both Best and Stevens arranging for a high-ranking anti-regime Wehrmacht general to be flown to London for secret talks. At stake, according to the SD double agents, was a military coup in Berlin. In fact, the entire episode was a brilliantly executed counter-intelligence operation, which led to the abduction in broad daylight of both Best and Stevens at the German–Dutch frontier near Venlo in eastern Holland on 9 November 1939.

News of the episode, which was to become known as the Venlo incident, did not reach The Hague for some hours. The contact with this alleged branch of the German underground was so secret that only one other member of the MI6 station, Stevens's deputy, Lionel Loewe, knew the full details: Loewe was the MI6 liaison officer with the Netherlands military intelligence service, and he was actually in the office of Major General Johan van Oorschot when the Dutch director of military intelligence learned of the catastrophe. Not only had van Oorschot been consulted by Stevens, but Dutch military intelligence

OPPOSITE: A modern reconstruction of the abduction.

had approved the rendezvous and assigned a Dutch liaison officer, Lieutenant Dirk Klop, to act as an observer. However, Klop had been fatally wounded by a German bullet during the struggle at the frontier, and both Best and Stevens were apparently alive and under interrogation at Düsseldorf. Furthermore, the so-called German resistance cell that they had been negotiating with Stevens continued to communicate with The Hague station by the transmitter provided at the outset by MI6.

MI6's London headquarters at 56 Broadway was thrown into turmoil over the incident. Conflicting reports poured into Menzies's office in Queen Anne's Gate, while the neutral Dutch government tried to disassociate itself from any involvement in espionage. The facts, which were established after the war by a Dutch parliamentary commission and an MI6 inquiry, were that Best and Stevens had been manhandled over the border into Germany by an SD team led by Walter Schellenberg and Alfred Naujocks. Throughout the same afternoon the two British officers underwent a preliminary questioning, and it was during this interrogation, according to Karl Ditges, the SS translator present, that Best mentioned the existence of the Z organization for the first time.

The immediate consequence of the affair in The Hague was the virtual closure of the MI6 station. All the PCO staff was instructed to suspend their work on the assumption that all their current agents and operations had been compromised.

Dansey's first reaction to the news of Venlo was to blame John Hooper, who had originally been dismissed from The Hague station in 1936, after which he had been approached by Hermann Giskes of the Abwehr. When Hooper later confessed to this, Dansey had wanted to deal with his ruthlessly, but was over-ruled.

Best and Stevens were suspected by MI6 of having provided their captors, under duress, with a mass of detail about the Secret Intelligence Service The Nazis displayed considerable skill in handling their prisoners and never once gave them the opportunity

to compare notes and thus minimize the impact of their answers. The two men were kept separate and each believed the other was responsible for providing their interrogators with the basis of their apparently extensive knowledge of the British intelligence agency. It was only some years after the war that another MI6 traitor, Dick Ellis, was identified as having sold information to his Abwehr contacts in pre-war Paris.

After the war, Best and Stevens were repatriated and debriefed by both MI5 and MI6 when each admitted to having been candid with the SD, and it was decided not to take any further action against them. Stevens took up a translating job with NATO and eventually retired to Brighton, where he died in 1965. Best became a bankrupt, but won a campaign to receive compensation for his imprisonment from the post-war German government. The British government opposed the inclusion of his name on the list of those who had suffered at the hands of the Nazis, but Best eventually received an award of £2,400 in 1968. He died bankrupt in 1978 at Calne in Wiltshire, aged 93, having published his memoirs, *The Venlo Incident*, in 1950.

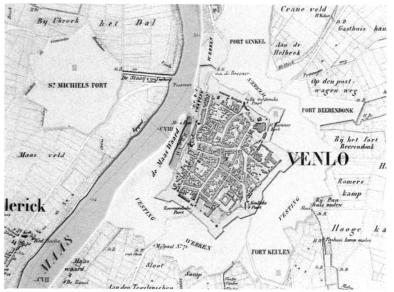

ABOVE LEFT: The Sicherheitsdienst chief, Reinhard Heydrich, who supervised the operation in retaliation for an attempt on the life of Adolf Hitler in a Munich beer cellar.

LEFT: A map of the Dutch town of Venlo, almost surrounded by German territory.

OPPOSITE: Walter Schellenberg, the shrewd SD counter-intelligence specialist who spent weeks developing a link to MI6 in The Hague by posing as an anti-Nazi Luftwaffe officer.

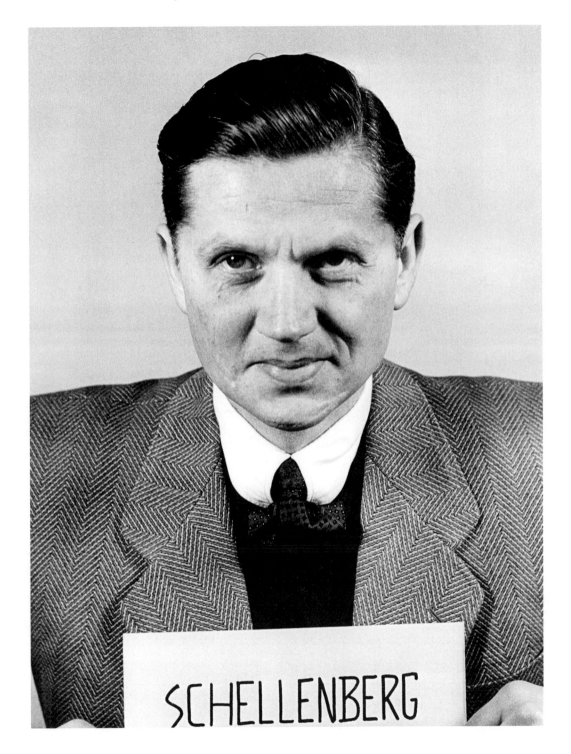

14. KURT LUDWIG

THE ABWEHR'S MAN IN THE UNITED STATES

A VICTORY FOR CENSORSHIP

Born in Freemont, Ohio, in December 1903 but taken to Germany in 1909, Kurt Ludwig returned to the United States in 1925, where he remained for the next eight years. Ludwig was an German intelligence officer who was arrested while on a mission in Austria in February 1938. He was released soon afterwards, following the Nazi annexation of Austria, and in March 1940 arrived in New York, where he established an extensive spy-ring, which he ran from his rented rooms in Ringwood, Queens, operating as an exporter of leather goods. This commercial cover provided him with a pretext to correspond with supposed customers in Madrid and Lisbon.

The existence of Ludwig's organization became known to the Federal Bureau of Investigation (FBI) when his reports, written in secret ink and concealed in innocuous letters addressed to neutral countries in Europe, were detected by a British Imperial Censorship scrutineer, Nadya Gardner, in Bermuda. This was where the transatlantic mails were routinely inspected at the Hamilton Princess Hotel. They were signed "Joe K", but the FBI would eventually identify Ludwig as the author from clues

Princess Hotel, Bermuda.

ABOVE: The Hamilton Princess Hotel in Bermuda, which accommodated the Imperial Censorship examiners who inspected all the transatlantic mail and initiated the investigation of the mysterious "Joe K".

contained in the correspondence and information recovered from a notebook found on the body of a German courier, Ulrich von der Osten, who died in Bellevue Hospital in New York on 19 March, having been hit by a taxi in a traffic accident in Times Square, Manhattan, the previous day. His companion had been seen to grab a briefcase and slip away into the crowd of pedestrians.

The incident had attracted attention because initially the victim was thought to be Don Julius Lopez Lido, a courier attached to the Spanish consulate and currently resident at the Taft Hotel, but routine police inquiries showed the notebook entries were written in German, and the hotel room was found to contain maps, aircraft production statistics and other suspicious military data, so the information was passed on to the FBI.

A further "Joe K" intercept revealed a reference to a road accident involving JULIO, and this assisted in identifying Lido as an alias adopted by von der Osten, who had arrived in the United States from Shanghai via Japan and Hawaii only a month earlier. He was a senior Abwehr officer, travelling on a false Spanish passport, who had had operated in Castile and Burgos throughout the Spanish Civil War. He was considered one of the Abwehr's few experts on America, with members of his family already in the United States, including his brother Carl Wilhelm, who was living in Denver and identified the body. Von der Osten had already earned an FBI file as he had previously appeared on the periphery of an earlier double agent case, involving a naturalized American, William Sebold, who had been coerced into assisting the Abwehr.

One of the items in von der Osten's notebook was a telephone number for a couple, David and Lori Harris, which matched a reference in the Joe K letters to "Uncle Dave" and "Aunt Lori". This clue led the FBI straight to their nephew Kurt, known as Fred, whose handwriting was identical to Joe K's.

Accordingly, Ludwig was placed under surveillance and watched as he visited the New York

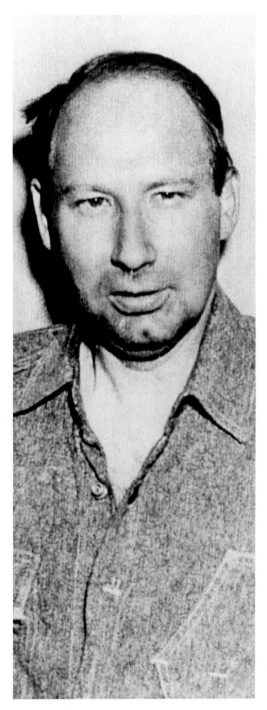

ABOVE: Kurt Ludwig, the Abwehr spy arrested by the FBI in Spokane in August 1941.

ABOVE: The federal prison on Alcatraz Island in San Francisco Bay where Ludwig served his sentence before he was deported to Germany in 1953.

Daily Express

No. 12,890   Wednesday, September 17, 1941   One Penny

LENINGRAD Shock troops and Home Guards make three successful attacks against the Germans. River islands are among positions recaptured.

ANKARA next capital on Hitler's list, is believed to be imminent war. German attack on Turkey may come any day.

BUDAPEST rejoices over news that Hungarian troops are coming home from front, and Hungary's part in Russian war is to be "reviewed."

ROME loses its immunity from air raids, given by Britain, as result of Axis bombing of Cairo, where 39 civilians have been killed and 93 injured.

TURKEY

The Express reporter who told you this—

STALIN GIVEN A WEEK
To choose—surrender or fight

Express Correspondent
GERMAN FRONTIER, Tuesday.

JUNE 25 is deadline for Stalin's capitulation to German demands for control of the Soviet's food and material resources, it was reported in Germany tonight.

From the Front Page, Daily Express, June 19, 1941 . . . Germany invaded Soviet Russia on June 22

Now tells you this—

Express Correspondent
ON THE GERMAN FRONTIER, Tuesday.

FROM the same high source which gave me the news of Germany's impending attack on Russia I am now informed that Turkey is in imminent danger of invasion.

Berlin has denied persistent reports of a coming German offensive in the East through Turkey. But the fact remains that heavy concentrations of troops and war material are stationed in Bulgaria.

Also, for no specific reason, Bulgaria last Sunday called up three new classes of men, giving them only five hours in which to answer the call.

Germany is making low progress on the Odessa front and the drive to the Caucasus over Russian territory will and winter conditions rapidly approach.

Urgent need

The German need to reach the oilfields very soon is urgent.

Rumania talks continue in Ankara. Dr. Clodius is doing his best finally to draw an agreement with Turkey before the British delegation gets a look in.

But in a regional exchange of goods the only reason for Dr. Clodius's visit is to draw raw material from Turkey, and the British delegation is here to prevent it.

10 panzer divisions
on Turk frontier

Express Foreign Expert

ANKARA reports that between eight and ten panzer divisions are already occupying all key points along the Turco-Bulgarian frontier.

I am informed that during the week-end German staff officers arrived in Sofia from Berlin, and the Russian front to discuss army supply problems with the Bulgarian Government.

It seems that not only a brigade is to used as the jumping-off point, but the Bulgaria army is to be dragged in also.

My information is that two fully equipped Bulgarian divisions are waiting on the Greek border, via two German divisions are facing the Turkish frontier in Eastern Thrace. The Germans have the usual corps of specially trained paratroops.

24 airfields

The Nazis have laid two dozen airfields in Bulgaria, all considerable numbers of Messerschmitts and Stukas are concentrated there.

They have now a Black Sea fleet at Varna and Constanza, Bulgarian and Rumanian ports which Admiral Raeder, Hitler's Commander-in-Chief, has turned into naval bases.

Co-ordinated with his fleet, on the other side of the Dardanelles, an Q-boats and X-boats which Raeder has ensconced into Greek ports from the ports he put.

Parallel with this military activity on land and at sea, the Nazis have started up their usual propaganda campaign pertinently to creating another century.

Wants the Straits

Satisfied neutrality has been the Turkish watchword. This has supposed Germans from passing out resources thus Turkey intends coming into the war on the side of Britain and Russia.

Passage through the Dardanelles would not be enough for Hitler.

He wants to gain entire control of the Straits and prevent any possibility of Russia or British flags flying through the Dardanelles.

All the signs point to Turkey becoming a new battlefield in the near future.

Frau Buggins speaks her mind

And all Germany listens

EXPRESS RADIO REPORTER

IN Germany she's known as Frau Wernicke, the shrill-voiced, truculent, irrepressibly fearless Berlin housewife who Speaks Her Mind. At the B.B.C. where she broadcasts once a fortnight, she's known as a gifted German ex-actress whose real name must remain a secret.

To Dr. Goebbels she's a major headache, because Frau Wernicke's monologues are rapidly becoming the rage among German listeners.

She's a kind of German Mrs. Buggins. She flops panting into a shelter and wheezes (in German): "Lawks, that was a close one, that was. The R.A.F. on the job again . . ."

And when the shelter marshal threatens dire penalties she belies: "I'm not afraid of 'em—I've been in concentration camp, I have. I'm up to your tricks. . . ."

'NOT LIKELY'

At the cinema she's vociferous in protest. Disregarding the 'risks' of a annoyance, Berlin audience, she says: "In the old days you could see a good cry at the movies. Now it's nothing but victories and heroes."

An advertisement flashes on the screen for radio sets. Snaps Frau Wernicke: "Radio sets! What for, I'd like to know. They tell me, they won't let you mill tune in to put in to foreign stations."

She nudges her husband—Fritz-like the war you could pot a rival about of offensives at the pictures—now you're fed on pathos and culture, and more culture—"

Each broadcast she's in a different mind—her husband, as a the part; or a gent's wanting or watching one of the processions and whistle she has a straight job reclaiming Gestapo snooping—Goebbels propaganda and coated news bulletins.

She says that every German housewife must want to say, but doesn't. They'll be another tirade from Frau Wernicke next Saturday at 3 and 7 pm.

E^IGHTEEN-YEAR-OLD LUCY BOEHMLER, who left Germany seven years ago, has pleaded guilty in New York to spying secrets from American soldiers and passing them on to a master spy and to the German gestapo—on account of completing gallows—are accused of completing to violate the U.S. Espionage Act.

LENINGRAD GOES OUT TO FIGHT

Bombers smash Nazi pontoons and airfields

Express Staff Reporter E. D. MASTERMAN

STOCKHOLM, Wednesday morning.

LENINGRAD'S shock troops went into battle yesterday and hurled the enemy back as the German High Command warned the city that no humane consideration could count any more since the entire population was fighting against the invader.

Three bitter, hand-to-hand counter-attacks from Leningrad were described by the Russians last night.

In one, river islands being used as a jumping-off ground against the city were recaptured.

In another, a whole German regiment was wiped out and big tanks put to flight.

This morning's Moscow communiqué gives only one new detail of yesterday's fighting.

It says that Russian planes bombed pontoon bridges over the Neva in the Ukraine, where the Germans claim to be advancing on a wide front across the River Dnieper, with advance units deep into the steppes leading to the Crimea.

Savage blows

The run of the communiqué reports savage fighting along the whole battlefront, with the Red Air Force battering at enemy positions and enemy airfields.

It is also announced that another huge German convoy was sunk in an E-boat attack on Leningrad's flank—making three in one day.

Leningrad should unite save Petrograd yesterday (a boy have been fighting since June 9 under extremely hard conditions.

CRISIS?

According to a report from Rome, a Government crisis is expected in Hungary.

Hungarian, Slovakia and Croatia are reported to be sitting in a secret conference on Brzeźczyce to make territorial claims against one another.

They are said to be planning a military alliance to support Hitler.

Hungary is reported to have appealed by Hitler to pos us and the Bessaina conspiracy—Exchange and Reuter.

The Archduke Otto, Pretender to the throne of Hungary, said in a speech at Willesden yesterday that a strong movement was being started to unite all Hungarians of the world of the British Empire. There was no possible understanding with Hitler.

15 die in Eireann army explosion

FIFTEEN men were killed near Waterford yesterday in an explosion of the Eireann Army were killed and 50 injured when an ammunition dump accidentally exploded during exercises at the Glen of Imaal, in the Wicklow Hills, yesterday. Members of the Engineering Corps were carrying out tests with explosives when the mine went off.

HUNGARY TRIES TO GET OUT OF WAR

ZURICH, Tuesday.

HITLER has agreed that it is necessary to withdraw Hungarian troops from the Russian front.

Hungary's part in the future conduct of the war will now be fully reconsidered.

These facts were announced to the Hungarian Parliament by Dr. Bardossy, in reply to a recent visit to Germany, and Budapest messages today.

This news is laden with delight in Budapest, as Hungarian troops have been fighting since June 22 under extremely hard conditions.

← BACK PAGE. COL. FOUR

Bombs for Rome?

Axis planes raid Cairo, defy British warning

Express Air Reporter BASIL CARDEW

CAIRO was bombed early yesterday. Will the R.A.F. now carry out systematic bombing of Rome, fulfilling the British Government's warning made last April?

The warning stated that if Cairo or Athens (but then in Axis hands) were bombed, we would begin "a systematic bombing of Rome which would continue in convenient until the end of the war."

It apparently deterred the Germans and Italians from carrying out threats to bomb these cities, last year until the raid was made on Cairo area, killing 39 civilians and injuring 93.

The Germans say the raid was on a British airfield.

Cairo is a holy city of the Moslems, and capital of a country which is not at war.

Egypt has never declared war on either Germany or Italy—British troops are in Egypt under special treaty rights.

ITALIAN PLOT

When plans were made last April for the R.A.F. to attack Rome, to fear the British warning was unheeded, and plans were drawn that the greatest care must be taken not to touch the Vatican City.

We knew that no Italian squadron was being held ready to drop captured British bombs on the Vatican City should a British raid on Rome take place.

R.A.F. bomber pilots have been striving for some time to make a smash at Mussolini's headquarters. They read the R.A.F. bombed Rome is not Rome is a holy city a new industrial zone in the central in Rome, and that the Italian firms have already applied for factory sites there.

WINS WINNERS ON SATURDAY

THE WINS competition, started by the Daily Express to find the best girl at the nursery, is now being judged.

Mrs Caroline Haslett, president of the Women's Engineering Society, Miss C. A. about fame of leading through the Cabinet, Mesmark and face, Savings Certificate cheeks, and on Saturday the prize-winners will be announced. The prizes are:—
1st—50 Savings Certificates
2nd—25 Savings Certificates
3rd—15 Savings Certificates

ALL SILENT ON THE LIBYA FRONT

SILENCE fell suddenly on the war in the Middle East last night.

The usual nightly communiqués from O.H.Q. in Cairo and Middle East had not reached London up to early today. Unofficial news from Cairo referred to "great activity" in the frontier area.

There was a similar silence at Cairo O.H.Q. on December 6 last year, the day the Imperial armies began their big advance which carried them right across Cyrenaica.

A German High Command spokesman said on the Berlin radio last night:—

"A full-scale British offensive in Libya must be expected."

"Weather conditions have improved and activity is likely to flare up at any moment."

The British are searching for some action which will relieve the Soviets."

GERMAN BALTIC INVASION SMASHED

MOSCOW, Tuesday.—Second German attempt to land troops by air and sea on Island of Oesel, Red base in the Baltic, has been smashed, says Lovevsky, Soviet spokesman.

"After two days' fierce fighting, the bulk of enemy marine and air landing parties had been annihilated and the remainder thrown into the sea."—Tass.

ON, ON, ON!

Express Radio Station

"On and on we go" that von Nazi war reporter was shouting hysterically over Deutschlandsender radio last night when the "Merseyside boats" broke in saying:—

"On, on, on all over us be and bleeding."

De Gaulle back

General de Gaulle, Leader of the Free French, has returned to Britain after an absence of five months in Syria, the Sudan, Eritrea and Equatorial Africa.

"It's jam for us, thanks to you, Mr Barratt!"

"Well, I see you've got a good haul of blackberries," I said to this happy-looking couple whom I met out in the country, "and I hope they'll make nice jam. But I fail to see why you should thank me for it."

"Do you think I'd have got my husband to come out on an expedition like this if it hadn't been for you, Mr Barratt?" remarked his lady. "No! likely! Had it have said he couldn't face a long walk with feet like his!"

The husband smiled. "You've a lot to answer for, Mr. Barratt. Your bleached shoes are so comfortable that I've no excuse for staying indoors and getting broody."

And a jolly good thing, too! Hitler may have blacked us out but he can't make us blue so long as we've got fresh air and the freedom of the countryside. Of course, if you're a slave to your feet, the last thing you'll do is to take advantage of it. But if you walk the Barratt way—in good British shoes, built to support and protect your feet with natural ease, by Northampton's best craftsmen, you'll get health and cheerfulness into you on every possible occasion.

Don't forget to write to Headquarters, Northampton, if you're out of touch with a Barratt branch.

Walk the Barratt way

Barratts, Northampton, and branches all over the country.

SIX GERMANS SHOT DOWN

Bombers sank a patrol vessel of Holland yesterday and our fighters shot six Germans into the air off France. One of our own fighters and two of our fighters are missing.

Bombed by storm clouds and a leaden sun, Nevs overnight, bombs flaming columns and R.A.F. gave watchers on the south-east coast last night their most spectacular sight of the war.

R.A.F. were protecting barges around the occupied ports in France.

Bombs were dropped at an cost coast town last night. No casualties were reported.

First bombs were dropped on a land in England. No damage or casualties were caused.

Nazis report first U.S. flier captured

Listen list of R.A.F. prisoners in Germany, given by a German source last night, includes for the first time the name of an American, Sergeant Robert Thomas Wood, of Dallas, Texas.

Duke of Kent on air

The Duke of Kent will broadcast at six o'clock this evening in the Empire programme.

We enter Teheran today

BRITISH and Russian armies are expected to reach Teheran today to begin their task of cleaning up Axis Fifth Columnists. As the British troops neared the city last night the ex-Shah was driving out, by the same road, toward Isfahan.

—Story on Back Page.

Swedish vice-consul detained by Nazis

Express Radio Station

The Swedish vice-consul in Bordeaux is reported by Stockholm radio to have been detained by the German military authorities.

He is accused of travelling to and fro in the unoccupied parts of France with letters against censorship regulations.

He can sign for Roosevelt

To speed lease-lend

WASHINGTON, Tuesday.—President Roosevelt told his Press conference today that he had named Mr. Edward Stettinius jun. as special assistant who could affix the Presidential signature to lease-lend papers, as obstructing a declaration at the White House.

Added another concerning war appropriation for control of war weapon stored, he said another statement should not think there was only one materiality north and south, but one calm. There was no end.

Windsors to lunch with U.S. President

WASHINGTON, Tuesday.—The Duke and Duchess of Windsor will be guests of President and Mrs. Roosevelt at the White House on September 25.

They will be guests in Washington on a visit to the Duke's Canadian ranch.—Reuter.

THE BATTLE OF NOEL

For lead in Lord Louis film

By JONAH BARRINGTON

A BATTLE is going on over the choice of leading man for the new £150,000 film about the British Navy.

When I published the news that Noel Coward would play the part of Lord Louis Mountbatten, hero of the destroyers (both of Crete), an official denial was issued.

Nevertheless, I am now informed that a fight is still going on to pin Coward in the leading rôle. The argument against is based on a question of good taste and reputable and can it be an exhibition of the part of the Mountbatten.

There are two schools of thought:
1. Those who support it.
2. Those who do not.

Those who do not support it argue that in the interest of the propaganda the role should not be taken by Mr. Coward. Lord Louis by will recognise a film by the name of someone equally well-known. The Navy could be best served by preserving him incognito of the British film standard should so well received as "Target for Tonight," which won universal acclaim because of all that is wrong in audibility.

Opponents say that it is wrong in audibility.

It is argued that it would be impossible to detach Mr Barry from his character which they felt the British public, even their a film production immediately. Another factor is that Coward is not enthusiastic over the idea. He is inclined to regard a film about Lord Louis as a personal friend as in bad taste.

It is intended as important that when documentary film of the British Navy should be as well received as "Target for Tonight," which won universal acclaim because of all that is wrong in audibility.

Shots at two more Paris Nazis

VICHY, Tuesday.—A German Army sergeant was shot and seriously wounded when he had walked early in the Boulevard de Strasbourg in the heart of Paris today. When travellers take taxis to Switzerland.

Later, several shots were fired at another German soldier as he was entering a Metro station. All the firers missed.

These shootings were apparently reply to the announcement yesterday that three French hostages had been shot by the Germans at Rouen after a Nazi officer had been shot there.—Reuter.

Fine in Straits

Weather in the Straits of Dover was fine last night, although heavy clouds hid the moon. The sea visibility north and the sea was calm. There was no mist.

Mr. Deeds meets Joe London—Page 2

ABOVE: Lucy Boehmler's conviction for espionage becomes *Daily Express* front page news in the UK.

docks and other military installations in the state. In May, he was trailed to Florida, accompanied by his young blonde secretary, Lucy Boehmler, and was seen to meet a contact, Carl Schroetter, in Miami. Schroetter, who was arrested in September 1941, had emigrated in 1913 and was the owner of a charter boat, *Echo of the Past*. He would be sentenced to 10 years' imprisonment.

In June 1941, when the newspapers reported on the FBI's arrest of another, unrelated German spy-ring in New York, headed by Frederick Duquesne, Ludwig suspended his network's activities and drove to Pennsylvania before heading to Wyoming and Montana, where he abandoned his car, in which a short-wave radio was found.

Ludwig was detained in a town near Seattle in August 1941 and seven others connected to the German–American ring were charged with espionage. They were a Jewish academic, Paul Borchardt, who claimed to have spied under duress in return for his release from Dachau; Rene Froehlich, a soldier based at Governor's Island, New York; a machinist, Karl Mueller; a housewife, Helen Mayer; Hans Pagel, aged 20; and Frederick Schlosse, aged 19.

The FBI concluded that the organization had been engaged in the collection of military information and industrial production figures which had been passed through a series of cut-outs and dead-drops to the German consulate-general where the janitor, an FBI informant, had found traces of Borchardt's reports in a burn-bag. Evidently von der Osten had been dispatched to take control of the network, but fate had intervened.

Because his espionage had been conducted before Germany had declared war on the United States, Ludwig received a prison sentence of 20 years in March 1942, and escaped the death penalty. Boehmler, who gave evidence against Ludwig, received a reduced sentence of five years' imprisonment. Ludwig served his sentence at Alcatraz and was deported to Germany in 1953.

Kurt Frederick Ludwig 1940

ABOVE: The FBI mugshot of "Joe K", the spy tracked across the United States after he had been compromised.

The most elusive member of the group was a German Jew, Theodor Lau, who had acquired Argentine citizenship and had acted as the network's paymaster. Codenamed BILL by the Abwehr, he appeared in numerous highly incriminating archived telegrams originating from Dietrich Niebuhr, the German naval attaché in Buenos Aires, and was tracked to Argentina before he was detained on 18 October 1946 as he returned to New York from Canada, having travelled from Rio de Janeiro to Vancouver.

Examination of his MI5 file disclosed that between 1938 and 1939 Lau had run a silk hosiery business in London's Hanover Square, and in July 1941 had been in Cape Town. At the FBI's request Lau's activities had been reviewed by MI5's Michael Ryde, Peter Ramsbotham and Desmond Vesey, and passed to Peter Wilson at MI6. Under interrogation, Lau confessed to special agents Thomas Spencer and Roy Barloga that he had set up Ludwig's spy-ring and had financed it through bank transfers from Argentina.

15. CODENAME SONIA

URSULA KUCZYNSKI, STALIN'S FAVOURITE SPY

COTSWOLDS CALLING MOSCOW

Codenamed SONIA by the Soviet military intelligence service (GRU), Ursula Kuczynski was a Soviet agent who worked under her own name in England, where her brother Jurgen led the German Communist Party (KPD) opposition to the Nazis, and in Switzerland where she helped run a wartime spy-ring.

Originally recruited to the GRU by Richard Sorge (see pages 86–91) in China, SONIA was first married to a German architect, Rudolf Hamburger, and moved with him to Shanghai in July 1930 when she was 23. Kuczynski had already developed her politics through a period working in New York, where she had helped run the Henry Street Settlement with the legendary Lillian Wald to accommodate poor Jewish families.

Upon her arrival in China, Ursula had been introduced to Sorge by his lover, the American writer Agnes Smedley and, beginning in November 1930, he transformed her into a GRU professional. By the time she reached Switzerland, accompanied by her two children in December 1939, she had divorced Hamburger and was a full-time Soviet agent working in support of a network based in Geneva headed by Alexander Rado. Ostensibly the proprietor of a map-publishing business, Rado supervised GRU operations in Italy and acted as an intermediary for the Soviet embassy in Paris.

In Geneva, she lived with Paul Boettcher, a former member of the KPD's central committee who had fled to Switzerland when the Nazis seized power in Germany. Her role was to run the two British volunteers, Alexander Foote and Leon Beurton, both veterans of the International Brigade,

ABOVE LEFT: Jurgen Kuczynski, head of the German Communist Party in England and reluctant intermediary for the GRU in London.

ABOVE RIGHT: Ursula Kuczynski, codenamed SONIA, the GRU agent sent to England to act as a courier for the London *rezidentura*.

ABOVE: The insignia of the Red Army.

to whom she taught the rules of *konspiratsia*. She also handled Rachel Duebendorfer, a Polish KPD activist who had acquired Swiss citizenship through a marriage of convenience, and then had found employment as an interpreter and typist with the International Labour Organization in Geneva.

Under instructions to obtain a British passport, Ursula married Beurton, a member of the Communist Party of Great Britain (CPGB) whose French father had become a naturalized British subject and had been killed on the Western Front in 1914. Then, having acquired British citizenship, she moved to Oxfordshire in December 1940, and was assigned the task of managing several sources who had offered information to the CPGB.

Although Ursula maintained that she was in direct communication with Moscow by radio, it is clear from the VENONA decrypts (the Soviet ciphers intercepted by Britain and America – see pages 158–63) mentioning BRION (believed to be Boris Shvetsov of the GRU's London *rezidentura*) dated 31 July 1941 that she had met someone working under the codename IRIS the previous day to discuss wireless schedules and her finances.

Ursula's version of events has it that before leaving Geneva she had been given instructions on how to make contact with her local controller, Sergei. She met him near Hyde Park not far from Marble Arch. She never disclosed, and probably never knew, Sergei's true identity, concealed in the VENONA traffic by the codename IRIS.

Ursula was acquainted with several senior Labour politicians, and was on good terms with the British ambassador to Moscow, Sir Stafford Cripps. She also claimed to have acquired military documents, which she passed to Sergei.

Among those who supplied information to Ursula were her brother Jurgen, who went to work for the Office of the Strategic Bombing Survey in London as an economist, and Erich Henschke, who acted as an intermediary with Joseph Gould, an OSS officer assigned the task of recruiting Germans willing

ABOVE: Allan ("Alexander") Foote was recruited by the GRU for a mission to Germany and Switzerland.

to be parachuted back into Germany. In addition, Ursula recruited two Britons, an RAF officer she called "James", who was a welder by trade, and a radio operator, "Tom"; both of them were ideologically motivated to spy.

Probably SONIA's most important role was to act as courier for the atomic physicist Klaus Fuchs, then based at Birmingham University (see pages 164–69). They first met at a café in Birmingham in October 1942, and went on to hold a regular rendezvous in the Oxfordshire market town of Banbury every three or four months. They met six times, but Fuchs never learned her true name.

The Beurton husband and wife team were obliged to suspend joint operations while Leon served with his regiment, and he was not demobbed until February 1947. While operating alone, Ursula was disconnected by Moscow Centre from "the summer or autumn 1946".

ABOVE: Jurgen Kuczynski at his large post-war home in East Berlin.

GRU

Formally the Main Intelligence Directorate of the Red Army's General Staff, the GRU was founded by Leon Trotsky in November 1918 and operated independently of the Communist Party's intelligence apparatus. During the Cold War few GRU personnel defected to the West, so little was known about its internal structure, staff or senior management. After the collapse of the Soviet Union in 1991, the GRU continued as an elite military organization, unreconstructed, and in March 2018 took ruthless action to silence a former mole, Colonel Sergei Skripal, who had been released from a long Russian prison sentence as part of an international spy exchange (see pages 196–198).

WHO WAS IRIS?

In Russian IRIS means either "the flower" or "toffee". IRIS appears only twice in the VENONA texts, the first in fragments of a report dated 1 August 1940 giving an account of IRIS's recent visit to Liverpool, describing Blenheim bombers at an airfield. Several French warships in port had been noted, and the military nature of the observations, coinciding with other VENONA traffic, strongly suggests that IRIS was a staff member of the GRU's *rezidentura*.

In September 1947, based on information from Alexander Foote, who had defected to the British, MI5's Jim Skardon and Michael Serpell visited SONIA at The Firs, her ramshackle cottage in Church Lane in the village of Great Rollright, but at that encounter she had simply confirmed that she had not been in touch with the Soviets since her arrival in England in 1941, and declined to co-operate further. She reported this encounter to Moscow immediately, and another identical confrontation in April the following year, but MI5 never linked her to Fuchs until long after she had fled to East Germany on 27 February 1950, three weeks after the newspapers had announced Fuchs's arrest.

MI5's subsequent investigation of SONIA revealed that much of her family had been engaged in espionage. Her brother Jurgen had been one of Fuchs's contacts and had directed him to the GRU *rezidentura* at the London embassy when he had first offered to spy, but her sister Brigitte Lewis had handled Foote in St John's Wood in September 1938, soon after his recruitment. Her autobiography, *Sonia's Story*, was published in 1977, and she died in Berlin in 2000, soon after the death of her husband.

OPPOSITE: Ursula Kuczynski in her role as the author Ruth Werner. In reality, She lived in abject poverty in East Berlin with her English husband who was crippled by arthritis.

16. RICHARD SORGE

SOVIET SPY IN THE FAR EAST

JOURNALISTIC COVER

Born in Baku, on the Caspian, to a German oilfield engineer, Richard Sorge was a Soviet Intelligence Officer who worked undercover as a journalist. He was wounded twice while fighting with the Kaiser's forces during the First World War. He then became an active member of the German Communist Party (KDP), attending its Second Congress in 1921 as an official delegate, and contributed to a leftist newspaper, *The Voice of the Mineworkers*, based at Solingen in the Ruhr. Sorge attended Aachen University, wrote several economic textbooks and joined a Soviet intelligence network in around 1924. He appeared to have cut his links with the KPD and with his schoolteacher wife Christiane, who was later to emigrate to the United States. In reality, he went to Moscow for training and reportedly attended a clandestine radio course.

Sorge's first overseas mission appears to have taken him to Hollywood, where he wrote articles on the American movie industry for a German magazine. In 1929 he was interviewed by a Metropolitan Police Special Branch detective in London which, although a routine encounter at his hotel concerning the registration of aliens, had the effect of terminating his visit. This visit appears to have lasted ten weeks, supposedly for the innocent purpose of studying British politics and economics.

Sorge later turned up in Shanghai working undercover as correspondent for *Sozialogische Magazin*, working with a radio operator, Seber Weingarten. Here, he developed a large intelligence network for the GRU and was responsible for the recruitment in 1930 of Ursula Kuczynski (see pages 82–85), her husband Rudolph Hamburger and

ABOVE: Richard Sorge (left) in Berlin's Lazarett Lankitz military hospital recovering from shrapnel wounds to his leg in July 1915.

OPPOSITE: Richard Sorge in the uniform of the Third Guards Field Artillery Regiment, aged 20.

Пролетарии всех стран, соединяйтесь!

3.

Буква алфавита

Хамовнич. район
(наименование организации)

Член ВКП(б.)

УЧЕТНАЯ КАРТОЧКА

1. Фамилия *Зорге. (Шварц)*

Имя и отчество *Ика. Рихардович.*

2. Пол *Мужской.* 3. Год рождения *1895.*

4. Народность *Немец.* 5. Родной язык *Немецкий.*

6. Социальное положение *служащий*

7. Основная профессия до вступления в ВКП(б.) *не имел.*

Число лет работы по этой профессии

Работал ли по основной профессии по найму или как ремесленник, кустарь и т. д.

8. Образование
   { а) общее *нар. школу и средне-учебн. завед.*
   { б) специальное *окончил. У-т.*
   { в) политическое

9. Время вступления в кандидаты

10. На какой стаж принят

11. Время перевода или приема в члены *с 1925.*

12. № { кандидатской карт.
       { членск. билета *78809 0049927*

13. Какой организацией принят
    { а) в кандидаты
    { б) в члены

14. Состоял ли раньше в ВКП(б.), когда и причины исключения или быбытия *нет*

15. Принадлежность к другим партиям (каким и когда) *с Неза-висимой С.Д. партии Германии с 1917 по 1919 г., с 1919 по 1925 г. с К.П. Германии.*

16. Принадлежность к ВЛКСМ

Карточку не мните и не сгибайте!

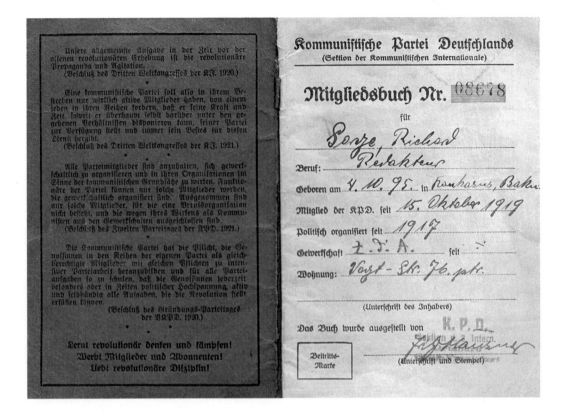

ABOVE: Sorge's German Communist Party membership card.
OPPOSITE: The spy's Communist Party registration card.

the veteran left-wing American journalist Agnes Smedley. Other contacts included Gerhart Eisler, later a senior Soviet intelligence officer in the United States, and Ozaki Hozumi, the local correspondent of the Tokyo daily, *Asahi Shimbun*, who returned to Japan in 1932 and organized a separate network.

Sorge's network in Shanghai was one of several parallel organizations that had been established by the Soviets, and scrutinized by the International Settlement Police, in which the British ran a Special Branch. Connections between various Far Eastern Communist Parties were routinely monitored. In June 1931 a raid on a man named Ducroux, a French member of the Communist Party in Singapore, led to the discovery of an address in Shanghai for the Comintern's (Communist International's) regional representative, Hilaire Noulens.

Noulens worked as a languages teacher, but a search of his home revealed identity papers, including Canadian and Belgian passports, in nine different names. At first the police believed him to be a Swiss, Paul Ruegg, who had been a prominent member of the Communist Party until 1924 when he had disappeared to Moscow, but Noulens did not admit to this. He and his wife Gertrude were handed over to the Chinese authorities for trial, and at a court martial in Nanking in October 1931 he was sentenced to death and his wife given life imprisonment.

After a long campaign for their release, conducted by an international defence committee, in which

ABOVE: Colonel Eugen Ott, the German military attaché in Tokyo who appointed Sorge to his embassy post. He became friends with Sorge and trusted him, unaware of his undercover activities.

Agnes Smedley and Sorge played important roles, the couple were released in June 1932 and deported to the Soviet Union. However, during the period they were held in Shanghai, the international police had an unprecedented opportunity to study the contents of three steel trunks, which proved to be the Comintern's regional accounts for 1930–31. Using the Pan-Pacific Trades Union as a convenient front, Noulens had liaised with the Chinese Communist Party and run a clandestine system of couriers. He had also maintained contact with a range of political activists in Indo-China, Japan, Hong Kong and Malaya through various sub-agents. One of the agents was Gerhart Eisler, a German Communist contact of Sorge's.

When word spread that Noulens had been taken into custody Sorge left Shanghai, but returned soon afterwards, apparently confident that he had not been compromised. Although he discouraged Ursula Kuczynski from helping the Noulens campaign, so as to avoid compromising her, many of those who lent their support, including Smedley and Ozaki, were actively engaged in espionage.

Even though some of those with whom Sorge had worked in Shanghai were recalled to Moscow and disappeared in Stalin's purges, Sorge himself was undeterred, and in May 1933 travelled to Berlin to join the Nazi Party and to take a staff job with the *Frankfurter Zeitung*. Sorge's transformation into a local supporter of the regime was completed with his cultivation of the Reich propaganda minister Joseph Goebbels and his introduction to Hitler.

When Sorge arrived in Tokyo later in 1933 to set up an intelligence network, he did so as a respected German journalist equipped with authentic Nazi credentials. He was popular in the local expatriate community's club and established an extremely useful friendship with Colonel Eugen Ott with whom he had served in the same regiment during the First World War. An artillery expert on attachment to the Japanese Imperial Army, Ott was later appointed military attaché at the German embassy and in 1940 succeeded Herbert von Dirksen as ambassador. Apparently Ott never suspected his friend, and it was on his recommendation that Sorge became the embassy's press attaché, a post which gave him useful access to German diplomatic cables, upon which he reported to Moscow. Evidently neither the Foreign Ministry in Berlin nor the Gestapo raised any obstacle to Sorge's appointment, apparently vindication of the wisdom of the GRU's decision to allow Sorge to use his own name while operating as an illegal.

Sorge's network in Japan fell under suspicion in June 1941 following the arrest by the Japanese military police, the Kempei'tai, of Ito Ritsu, a prominent member of the Japanese Communist

ABOVE: Agnes Smedley, the firebrand Missouri-born revolutionary journalist who became Sorge's mistress in Shanghai in 1929.

ABOVE: Branko Vukelic, pictured with his Japanese wife. He was Sorge's photographer and died in 1945 while serving a life sentence for espionage.

Party. Under interrogation he implicated Miyagi Yotoku, an American-educated Japanese artist, and he in turn led the Kempei'tai to the journalist Ozaki Hozumi. By the end of October, 35 members of the ring were under arrest, including Sorge himself and his radio operator, Max Klausen, a KPD activist. Among others taken into custody were Branko Vukelic, a Yugoslav spy who represented the French magazine *La Vue*, and Sorge's Japanese mistress, Mikaya Hanako.

Sorge and Ozaki were hanged on 7 November 1944, leaving only the summaries prepared by their principal interrogator, Yoshikawa Mitsusada, for study by post-war Allied investigators. Vukelic died serving a life sentence in 1945, but Max Klausen survived his imprisonment and was repatriated to Vladivostok, where he was promptly re-arrested by the Soviet intelligence agency, the NKVD, and taken under escort to Moscow for interrogation and to face charges of duplicity.

17. BLETCHLEY PARK

BREAKING THE ABWEHR'S ENIGMA

TAPPING THE ETHER

Also known as Station X, Bletchley Park was the war station of the British Secret Intelligence Service. It was a large mansion close to the railway junction at Bletchley in Bedfordshire, almost midway between Oxford and Cambridge. Initially mobilized during the Munich crisis of 1938, the extensive estate accommodated a large staff of linguists and cryptanalysts employed by the Government Code and Cypher School. At the height of its activities, some 12,500 personnel worked there, in the house or in the many temporary wooden huts erected in the grounds, concentrating on encrypted enemy communications.

From before the outbreak of the war, German military communications were encrypted using Enigma machines. In outward appearance they were broadly like old-fashioned typewriters, but with a rotor mechanism and a plugboard that scrambled the letters, and a panel where the encrypted (or decrypted) letter lit up. Early breakthroughs achieved at Barnet by the Radio Security Service (RSS) against Abwehr hand ciphers encouraged resources to be devoted to traffic encrypted on the Enigma machine, and the world's first programmable analogue computer, the Colossus, was developed to race through the even more complex permutations of the 10-rotor Geheimschreiber machine. Although, at the end of the Second World War, the renamed Government Communications Headquarters (GCHQ) moved to Lime Grove, Eastcote, in west London, and then in 1953 to Benhall in Cheltenham, Gloucestershire, the organization retained a small training facility at Bletchley until 1985.

The first disclosures about the work undertaken at Bletchley were made in 1974, although there had been a few earlier somewhat speculative assertions concerning the compromise of U-boat communications and the pre-war French cryptographic attack on Enigma. In 1977, once the surviving former staff had been allowed to publicly discuss aspects of their work, Bletchley's full role could be put into its proper context, within a collaborative matrix of the "Y" services which intercepted the enemy's wireless traffic; the RSS which monitored illicit broadcasts; MI5, responsible for the management of double agents transmitting to the Continent; Bletchley, where the cryptographers, linguists and analysts studied the traffic; Dollis Hill, the laboratory researching technical solutions to cryptological challenges; and Whaddon Hall, as a secure distribution centre for passing the sanitized summaries over a secure network to the designated recipients. All these components played their part in the capture of enemy messages, the analysis of their content, and the delivery of vital news to the theatre commanders.

There were the other contributors, such as the National Cash Register Company of Dayton, Ohio, which manufactured the "bombes" designed to race through Enigma machine key permutations, and the U.S. Annexe on Nebraska Avenue in Washington, DC, which solved the German naval daily SHARK key and sent the solution over a landline to Bletchley.

OPPOSITE: German soldiers encipher a message on a Wehrmacht Enigma machine, the standard method of encrypting tactic communications.

ABOVE: Bletchley Park, purchased in 1938 as MI6's War Station, which accommodated the Government Code and Cipher School, Britain's principal cryptographic organization.

At the outbreak of war the clandestine transmission of a single MI5 double agent, codenamed SNOW (see page 117), enabled RSS to monitor the signals and watch them relayed on an Abwehr Enigma channel, which provided an opportunity to reverse-engineer the daily key setting. The surprise for the RSS interceptors was the scope of the key, which involved a single daily change that was applied across the entirety of the enemy's European networks. This meant that breaking the Hamburg Abwehrstelle traffic compromised the Madrid—Berlin channel too.

Access to the Abwehr's internal communications – codenamed ISK for the machine ciphers and ISOS for the hand ciphers – meant that a large analytical organization, designated MI6's Section V, was needed to card, translate and exploit the windfall. The more raw material that was collected, the greater the chances of engineering a counter-intelligence coup by identifying a spy or recruiting a double agent, which in turn served to compound production.

The initial early success with the Abwehr Enigma demonstrated what could be accomplished, and served to encourage work on Luftwaffe communications, which in turn led to work on German army and naval channels.

The development of a coordinated industrial-scale concentration on the Enigma, and the obvious, immediate benefits of the intelligence source to the authorized consumers, meant high-level support for Bletchley, with some of the more juicy morsels served daily to the prime minister by the MI6 chief. This led to more ambitious projects, such as the investment in Colossus (the first programmable

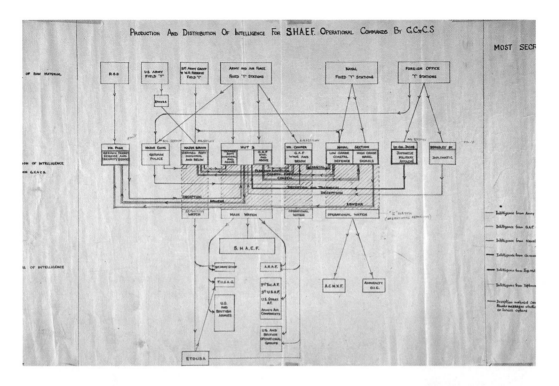

Production And Distribution Of Intelligence For S.H.A.E.F. Operational Commands By G.C.&C.S

MOST SECRET

ABOVE: An organisatonal chart illustrating the distribution of signals intelligence products to SHAEF components in 1944.

RIGHT: A three-rotor Enigma machine with the front flap down to reveal the plugboard.

computer), to tackle the Geheimschreiber online teletype machine, codenamed TUNNY, and even the Reich Foreign Ministry's supposedly unbreakable one-time pads, designated FLORDORA.

Bletchley Park was also in the forefront of new signals intelligence disciplines, such as traffic analysis, which enabled deductions to be made about the nature of certain traffic even when the content could not be read. Bletchley became the centre of a worldwide chain of intercept sites that engaged in such adjunct skills as direction-finding, radio finger-printing and call-sign analysis.

The tactical and strategic advantages supplied by Bletchley probably shortened the war by an estimated two years, and in the immediate post-war era continued to give successive British

governments an immense edge. Soviet military traffic, codenamed BOURBON, acted as a trip-wire with the prospect of alerting NATO to the unexpected mobilization of Soviet forces; VENONA exposed Soviet intelligence networks in the United States, Great Britain, Mexico, Sweden and Australia to the molehunters (see pages 158–63); Jewish Agency intercepts known as ISCOT and OATS revealed the Jewish Agency's covert links to terrorism in Palestine.

Bletchley ensured that signals intelligence became an indispensable part of policy-making, and Five Eyes agreements (of the intelligence alliance between Australia, Canada, New Zealand, the United Kingdom and the United States), based on wartime collaboration treaties to share the costs and benefits of the source with selected, English-speaking allies, would be enhanced to give truly global coverage to signal collection from the ether

ABOVE: The Colossus, the first programmable analogue computer, designed to solve the enemy's Geheimeschreiber online teletype machine cipher.

OPPOSITE: An Enigma "flimsy" or working decrypt of an intercept dated February 1945 from Berlin to Army Group Kurland on the Russian front, handled by Hut 3 cryptanalysts at Bletchley Park.

and from cable carriers. Even when Bletchley could not compete with the budgets available in the United States, it capitalized on its geographic assets in strategically located territories across the former British Empire. Ground-stations sprung up in Ascension, St Helena, Gibraltar, Malta, Cyprus, Palestine, Egypt, Masirah, Habbaniya, Diego Garcia, Delhi, Darwin, Hong Kong and Singapore. When the technology extended to satellites, more radome antennae were constructed to ensure continued access to international communications, and much the same happened at coastal terminals when fibre-optic cables were introduced in the digital age.

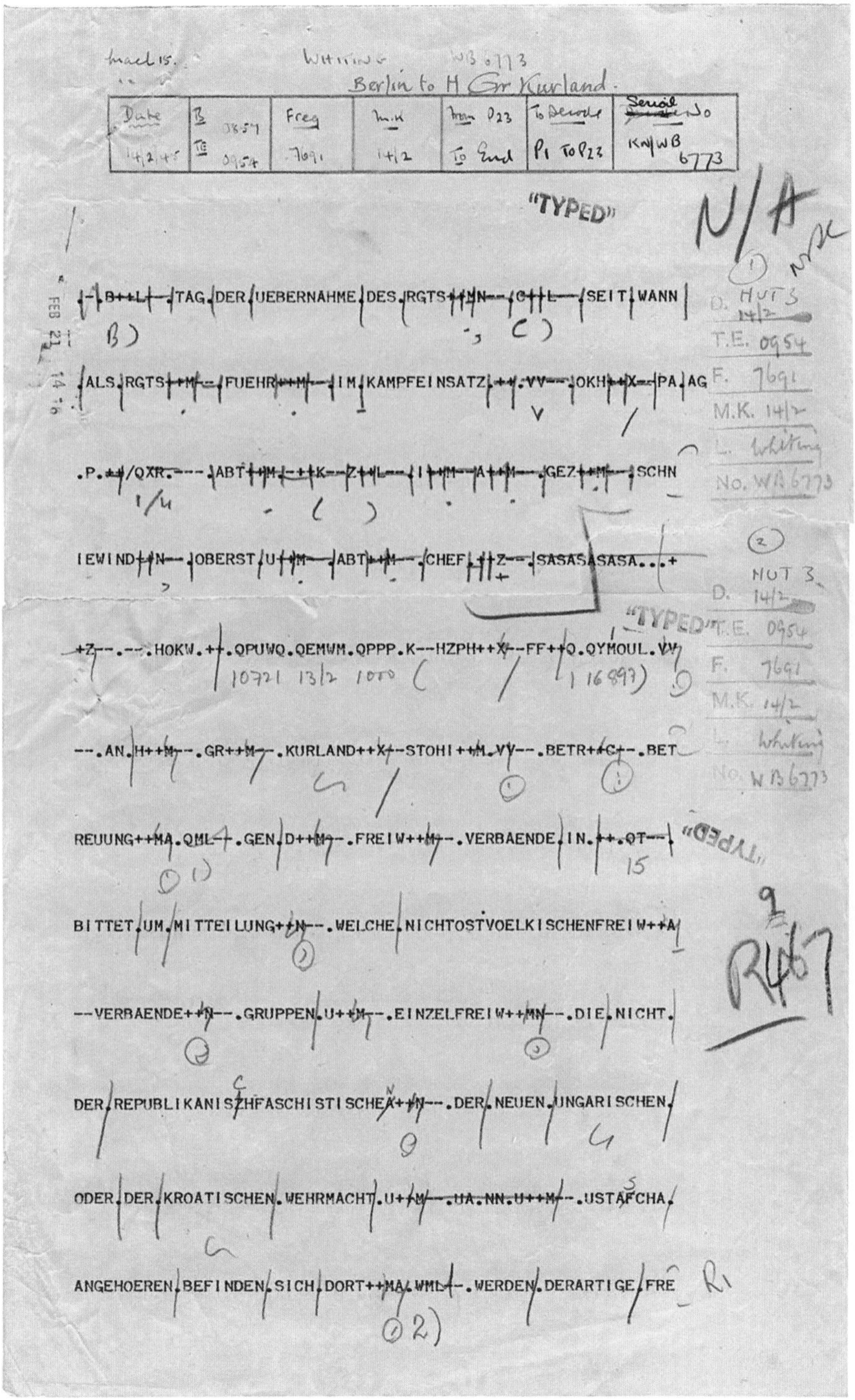

March 15.   WHITING   WB 0773
Berlin to H Gr Kurland.

Date	B T/B	Freq	M.K	From P23 To End	To Decode P1 To P23	Serial No
14.2.45	T/B 0854 T/E 0954	7691	14/2			KN/WB 6773

"TYPED"

N/A

|-|-|B++L|-|TAG.DER.UEBERNAHME.DES.RGTS++MN--.C+L-.|SEIT.WANN|

B)   -; C)

|ALS.RGTS++M--.FUEHR++M---.IM.KAMPFEINSATZ++V--.OKH++X--.PA.AG

.P.++/QXR.----.ABT++M++K--Z+.L--.|++M--A++M--.GEZ++M--.SCHN

1/4   - ( )

IEWIND++N--.OBERST.U++M--.ABT++M--.CHEF++Z--.SASASASASA...+

+Z--.-.HOKW.++.QPUWQ.QEMWM.QPPP.K--HZPH++X--FF++Q.QYMOUL.VV

10721 13/2 1000 ((16897)

---.AN.H++M--.GR++M--.KURLAND++X--STOHI++M.VV--.BETR++C+-.BET

REUUNG++MA.QML-+.GEN.D++M--.FREIW++M--.VERBAENDE.IN.++.QT--|

15

BITTET.UM.MITTEILUNG++N--.WELCHE.NICHTOSTVOELKISCHENFREIW++A

--VERBAENDE++N--.GRUPPEN.U++M--.EINZELFREIW++MN--.DIE.NICHT.

DER.REPUBLIKANISZHFASCHISTISCHEA++N--.DER.NEUEN.UNGARISCHEN.

ODER.DER.KROATISCHEN.WEHRMACHT.U++M--.UA.NN.U++M--.USTAFCHA.

ANGEHOEREN.BEFINDEN.SICH.DORT++MA.WML--.WERDEN.DERARTIGE.FRE

(2)

"TYPED"

D.	HUTS 14/2
T.E.	0954
F.	7691
M.K.	14/2
L.	Whiting
No.	WA 6773

(2)
D.	HUTS 14/2
T.E.	0954
F.	7691
M.K.	14/2
L.	Whiting
No.	WB 6773

R407

R₁

18. OPERATION MAGIC

U.S. DECRYPTION OF JAPANESE NAVAL CODES

CRYPTANALYSIS

Despite the ban imposed by Secretary of State Henry Stimson in October 1929 on the activities of the US Army's Black Chamber (see pages 44–47), MI-8's small team of five cryptanalysts had continued to work on what was termed "the Japanese problem" through the newly created Signal Intelligence Service (SIS) based at the Munitions Building in Washington, DC, in parallel with the U.S. Navy's Communications Security section designated OP-20-G. By 1935, after five years of toil, the SIS had achieved considerable success against RED, the "Type A" cipher machine used by Japanese naval attachés to encrypt messages transmitted to Tokyo by commercial carriers such as Western Union.

As the Axis began to take shape, the huge volume

of Japanese Foreign Ministry telegrams placed an increasing strain on the SIS's very limited resources, which boasted a staff of just seven, and an arrangement was made with OP-20-G to share the burden, with SIS handling traffic on even calendar days and the navy dealing with the odd days. This collaboration worked well, with SIS doubling its staff to 14, until March 1939, when the flow of decrypts suddenly ceased with the unexpected introduction of a more sophisticated replacement, the "Type B", codenamed PURPLE.

The PURPLE cipher generated by the Type B, of which only 25 models were built, resisted the decoders until 25 September 1940, when the first complete text succumbed and was distributed to the very limited group indoctrinated into the highly classified programme. The breakthrough occurred

ABOVE: Herbert O. Yardley (centre), surrounded by U.S. Army Signal Intelligence Service cryptanalysts at the Munitions Building in Washington, DC, in 1943.

OPPOSITE: The American reconstruction of the Japanese PURPLE machine, built without sight of an original.

after 20 months of pure cryptanalysis by a team led by William Friedman, who promptly suffered a nervous collapse.

Friedman's subordinate, Frank B. Rowlett, had been able to reconstruct the PURPLE cipher, and thereby develop a replica Type B machine, by exploiting two flaws in Japanese procedures. The first was a common error, known as the stereotype, which consisted of the stilted diplomatic language which convention dictated should begin and end individual telegrams. The predictable repetition of the pedantic phrase "I have the honour to inform your excellency" allowed the experts to glimpse the construction of particular messages, as did the Japanese habit of reproducing word for word the content of U.S. State Department communiqués. Since the cryptanalysts, among them Genevieve Grotjan, worked with copies of the original texts, they had little difficulty in retracing the process by which the Japanese had transformed the plain text into cipher. Similarly, a comparison between the embassy's diplomatic notes delivered by the

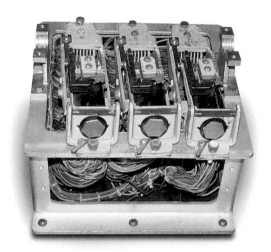

embassy to the State Department and the original encrypted texts proved profitable when it was realized that, for cultural reasons, the Japanese staff would not dare alter one word of the content.

Once Friedman had grasped the principles upon which PURPLE was based, Lieutenant Leo Rosen was able to build an electromagnetic device constructed from telephone exchange relays that duplicated the original device, and by January 1941, a model had been delivered to OP-20-G in Washington, DC, and another had been donated to Bletchley Park, which up until then had concentrated on the Japanese Navy's hand ciphers. Another is alleged to have been sent to the Far East Combined Bureau in Singapore.

The Allied window into the Japanese naval attaché circuits provided an invaluable source of intelligence, but it was an apparently routine seven-part cable, numbered 906, addressed to Colonel Hayashi in Berlin and Major Hirose in Helsinki, dated 6 October 1942 and translated early the following year, which proved to be crucial to solving some Russian systems. The message, written in an "emergency system", perhaps based on a book, was just one of a mass of enciphered communications between Japan and Europe that was intercepted by Allied radio operators at the Vint Hill Farms Station, outside Warrenton, Virginia, and passed

to a staff of 35 cryptographers and translators. It disclosed the results of a lengthy Japanese study of Soviet diplomatic and commercial traffic based on material exchanged between the embassies and consulates in Japan and Manchuria, and the Foreign Ministry in Kuibyshev.

An American trawl through previous naval attaché telegrams revealed that the first report on Soviet cryptographic systems had been transmitted to Tokyo on 1 July 1941 from Berlin, Stockholm, Helsinki and Hungary, and evidently since then, the Japanese had focused on the Moscow–Vladivostok link, as well as covering the diplomatic missions located at Seoul, Hakodate, and Dairen. According to the Japanese attachés, progress on the Soviet project had depended upon help provided in Helsinki by the Finnish authorities. Clearly, the Finns, exhausted by war with the Russians, had taken the strategic decision to cooperate with the Japanese, presumably in the hope of drawing Josef Stalin's attention to the Far East. The unlocking of PURPLE had long-term ramifications for gaining access to both Axis and Soviet communications.

OPPOSITE: William Friedman, the U.S. war Department's chief cryptographer, who created the Signal Intelligence Service in 1929.

ABOVE: The reconstruction of the Japanese "Type-B" cipher machine, constructed with telephone exchange relays.

19. OPERATION MINCEMEAT

HOW THE PLANTING OF MISINFORMATION
DIVERTED GERMAN ATTENTION FROM SICILY

TROJAN HORSE

The great Allied undertaking of 1943 was HUSKY, the invasion of Sicily. A cover-plan, BARCLAY, was devised to keep the Axis persuaded of a continuing threat in the eastern Mediterranean, and to provide evidence that the 12th Army was in Cairo, preparing for a move to Syria, and then the Balkans. The 12th Army was an invention, and was alleged to comprise 12 divisions, but in fact it was only ever five real divisions, with a further three, greatly inflated, divisions. Subsequent captured documents, prisoner interrogations and signals intercepts demonstrated that the enemy had completely accepted the 12th Army's existence.

In February and March 1944, when three of the 12th Army's real divisions were sent to Italy, they were replaced by notional divisions, and by April the 12th Army consisted of just two divisions and three brigades but, actually none of them was in any condition to engage in combat.

As well as the entirely fictitious reports generated by this operation, CHEESE, BARCLAY was supported by some genuine troop deployments. The plan worked, to the extent that the German reinforced the Balkans with an additional 10 divisions, and when the landings happened in Sicily there were only two German divisions there, which were taken entirely by surprise.

One of BARCLAY's more bizarre components was MINCEMEAT, a deception scheme dreamed up by MI5's Charles Cholmondeley. He originally suggested the idea of planting a corpse on the Germans bearing authentic-looking documents

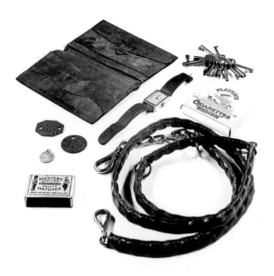

ABOVE: The "pocket litter" and briefcase leash assembled to give the body used in operation MINCEMEAT authenticity.

OPPOSITE: The corpse of "Major Martin" is prepared for delivery to HMS *Seraph*.

specially prepared to dupe the Abwehr, and suggested the codename TROJAN HORSE. As the project developed, it was dubbed MINCEMEAT.

On the face of it, the suggestion assumed a high degree of credulity on the part of the Germans but an incident shortly before, known as Operation TORCH, the invasion of North Africa in November 1942, indicated the ruse might work. A Catalina aircraft carrying a Free French courier, Lieutenant Clamorgan, had crashed on a flight from Plymouth to Gibraltar and his body had been washed up on the beach near Tarifa. Fortunately, TORCH was not compromised but the Frenchman was in possession of classified material and the Germans had obviously been passed various documents by the Spanish police before the body was surrendered to the Allies. The letters carried by the courier were not of vital importance but the behaviour of the Spanish suggested that MINCEMEAT might well achieve its purpose.

The plan was given all the necessary approvals and MI5 set about acquiring a suitable body that might undergo a cursory post-mortem examination and should be consistent with someone who had drowned.

A Naval Intelligence Division officer, Commander Ewen Montagu, liaised with MI5 to procure a cadaver and Sir Bernard Spilsbury, the Home Office pathologist, advised on what sort of body would be practical. He approached W. Bentley Purchase, the Westminster coroner, to select an unclaimed body from the Westminster mortuary. The body of a Welsh tramp named Glyndwr Michael was nominated and was put on ice while Cholmondeley and Montagu manufactured a plausible identity for "Major Martin RM" and engineered some sensitive documents for him to carry.

A homeless alcoholic, Michael had died after ingesting rat poison, but MI5 believed that a full autopsy was unlikely to be conducted in Spain, and the true cause of death would probably go undiscovered. Accordingly, on 17 April 1942, Jock Horsfall, Montagu and Cholmondeley loaded Major Martin into an MI5 30-cwt Ford and drove their charge up to Scotland to a submarine that was waiting to carry the body to the Spanish coast. The canister holding the corpse was packed with ice and bore the legend "optical instruments" for the benefit of the curious. It also contained a standard issue black government briefcase into which had been placed several bogus letters. The important one was from Admiral Mountbatten and was addressed to the Naval Commander-in-Chief Mediterranean, Admiral Cunningham. It explained that Major Martin was to deliver a personal note from the Vice Chief of the Imperial General Staff Archie Nye to "My dear Alex" (General Alexander). For good measure there was a further letter from Mountbatten to General Eisenhower concerning the preface to a pamphlet on joint operations that Eisenhower was to write.

To make Major Martin plausible, he was equipped with some ingenious "pocket litter", including an identity card bearing the photograph of an MI5 officer, Ronnie Reed, who resembled him, and the stub of a London theatre ticket, which provided confirmation of the date of the alleged air crash.

On 9 April HMS *Seraph* sailed from Greenock and 11 days later surfaced off Huelva in southern Spain to place Major Martin in the water. In due course the body was found on the beach alongside his rubber dinghy and all the evidence suggested that he was indeed an Allied courier whose plane had crashed into the sea. His official briefcase was still chained to his wrist. The British ambassador in Madrid, Sir Samuel Hoare, was duly informed of the discovery, though he was not let in on the deception, and indignantly demanded the return of the valuable letters. When eventually the naval attaché, Commander Alan Hillgarth, did receive the briefcase from the Spanish Ministry of Marine it was only after the sensitive documents had been photographed and passed on to the Abwehr.

The operation had been a success and ULTRA decrypts later showed that the MINCEMEAT documents had been accepted as genuine by the enemy. The Berlin High Command sent reinforcements to Sardinia and changed their ideas about the Allied intentions in the Mediterranean in accordance with BARCLAY's objectives.

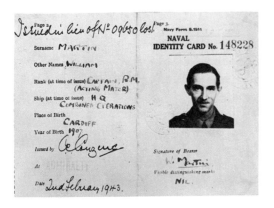

ABOVE: Major Martin's official identity card, bearing a photo of an MI5 officer, Ronnie Reed.

BELOW: HMS *Seraph*, the submarine commanded by Lieutenant Norman Jewell, assigned the task of delivering Major Martin's body to Huelva.

Wt. 22213/P6231. 16,500 pads. 9/42. A.G. Ltd. 51-5234.

POSTAGRAM OR MESSAGE

(Delete as necessary) OUT.

FOR WAR REGISTRY USE ONLY.

PASS TO:—

ADDRESSED

MOST SECRET

DATE 18. 5. 1943.

To:- N.A. Madrid (Personal)

From:- D.N.I. (Personal) No P77

MOST SECRET

IMPORTANT

SPECIAL ROUTE PASS BY HAND

SECRET.
CONFIDENTIAL
NON-CONFIDENTIAL.

Delete as necessary

Your 111925. Bag not yet arrived. Urgent that letters should be received earliest possible.

1. Was bag sent by air or sea?

2. Was the rubber dinghy washed up?

3. Evidence that operation successful but vital that no suspicion should be aroused.

N.I.D.12.   18 1213

Ext.193

Approved D.D.N.I. (H).

D.N.I. (only)

3 MAY 1943

CONFIDENTIAL   MESSAGE   021738B May
IN
From N.A. Madrid   DATE: 2.5.43
RECD: 0310

N.S.C. (OTP) by cable

Addressed Admiralty for D.N.I.

R.O. Huelva reports body identified as Major W. Martin R.M. card number 148228, has been washed ashore at Huelva. Death due to drowning probably 8 to 10 days ago. Spanish Naval Authorities have possession of papers found. Consul at Huelva has arranged funeral for noon today.

021738B

2nd S.L.
C.W.(Cas)Sect.(3)
N.A. 2nd S.L.(2)
N.(Stats)
M.D.G.
P.M.(2)
N.L.
Duty Capt.
Press Division
Admiral Munroe
A.G.R.M.
D.N.I.(5)
D.N.A. 4
5
9
D.N.A. Wills
S.W.R.

Bath
by courier

Sec. 20

"LIEUTENANT CLAMORGAN"

"Lieutenant Clamorgan" was the nom de guerre adopted by Louis Daniélou, the son of former minister Charles Daniélou. In March 1941 he had travelled to Tangier to join the Free French and had been enrolled in the Bureau Central de Renseignement et d'Action (BCRA) with responsibility for liaising with the British SOE and the U.S. OSS. On 25 September 1942, his aircraft from 202 Squadron Coastal Command crashed during a storm, killing the crew of seven and their three passengers. Daniélou, in possession of a British passport (improperly supplied by SOE) identifying him as "Charles D. Marcil", had been carrying BCRA documents which, according to ISOS decrypts, had been copied by the Spanish authorities and passed to the Abwehr. An inquiry was conducted by MI6's Guy Westmacott who reported that the BCRA had insisted that the papers had not been compromised. Nevertheless, the prime minister's intelligence adviser, Desmond Morton, told Churchill on 22 October that the incident had been the culmination of "incredible acts of folly" committed by the Free French, which had jeopardized British, American and Polish clandestine operations in North Africa. Another victim of the crash had been a 23-year-old naval officer, James Turner, who had been in possession of plans relating to TORCH, but his body had been delivered to Gibraltar intact, and scrutiny of ISOS intercepts on the Madrid–Berlin channel suggested that the operation had not been compromised.

ABOVE LEFT: A specious Admiralty signal to Madrid requesting further information, intended to add authenticity to the deception scheme.

LEFT: A message from the British naval attaché in Madrid reporting the recovery of Major Martin's body in Huelva.

20. OPERATION ANTHROPOID

THE ASSASSINATION OF HOLOCAUST ARCHITECT
REINHARD HEYDRICH AND THE DISASTROUS AFTERMATH

AN SOE ASSASSINATION

The British SOE's Czech Section, headed by Peter Wilkinson, was dogged by bad luck from the outset. Its first agent was supposed to be inserted on 16 April 1941. However, Otmar Riedl was dropped into Austria by mistake on Operation BENJAMIN and arrested for crossing the frontier illegally. Luckily, at the time of his capture, Riedl had already abandoned his equipment, so he was charged with nothing more serious than illicit border crossing, a relatively minor offence considering the penalties for espionage. Following the failure of BENJAMIN, Operation PERCENTAGE followed on 4 October, with Corporal Frantisek Pavelka being parachuted near Caslav with ciphers and a transmitter for delivery to the Czech resistance. He was arrested in Prague just three weeks later.

Despite this poor start, SOE was drawn into a project that originated with Edward Benes's government-in-exile to assassinate the Nazi "Reich-Protektor", the high-ranking SS officer Reinhard Heydrich. The precise circumstances in which this apparent change in policy came about is unclear, but generally such conduct was not regarded, at least in London, as being acceptable. In a not too dissimilar episode the RAF had protested in 1941 about an SOE-planned raid codenamed SAVANNA to ambush a bus in occupied France and kill Luftwaffe aircrew belonging to Bomber Unit 100 being driven to their airfield near Meucon. The Chief of the Air Staff, Sir Charles Portal, thought the proposal totally unacceptable. Again, in July 1943 objections were raised to Operation RAT

TOP: An identity medallion carried by all members of the Gestapo, engraved on the reverse with an individual number.

ABOVE: The hated Reichsprotektor of Bohemia and Moravia, Reinhard Heydrich, was selected for assassination by the Czech government-in-exile in London.

ABOVE: Heinrich Himmler (centre) confers with Reinhard Heydrich (second from right) and Heinrich Müller at Gestapo headquarters in Berlin.

WEEK, in preparation for which a list of senior German personnel, together with their French and Belgian collaborators, were singled out as targets for "liquidation". The submission from SOE was controversial, but went ahead nonetheless.

When the SOE team codenamed ANTHROPOID flew to Czechoslovakia from RAF Tangmere on 28 December 1941 accompanied by SILVER A and SILVER B, its objective was the assassination of the SS Obergruppenführer Heydrich in Prague. The plan was supposed to be executed on the Czech National Day, 28 October 1941. However, bad weather forced two postponements, so the team did not assemble in Czechoslovakia until late December.

Eventually, after further delays, a new date was set for 27 May 1942 and an ambush was prepared

as the Nazi was being driven in to Prague from the country mansion he occupied at Panenske Blezany. When his chauffeur-driven Mercedes-Benz approached a sharp bend on the outskirts of the city it slowed to negotiate the corner and as it did so a pair of the SOE men stepped into the road and attacked the open-topped limousine. The two SOE assassins were Czech paratroopers Sergeant Jan Kubis and Josef Gabcik from ANTHROPOID, with support from Josef Valcik and Adolf Opalka from OUT DISTANCE, two members of a three-man team which had arrived on 28 March.

At the vital moment Gabcik's Sten gun jammed but Heydrich was mortally wounded by a modified Mills grenade thrown by Kubis. Without waiting to see the results of their handiwork, the SOE men escaped the scene, only to be betrayed soon afterwards to the Gestapo by the third member of OUT DISTANCE, Karel Curda, who identified his comrades and their hiding place in the Karel Boromejsky Church in return for a reward. Cornered in the crypt, the SOE duo resisted the surrounding Germans until they ran out of ammunition, and died in a suicide pact. Curda alone survived the war, only to be hanged for treachery.

Heydrich was badly wounded by shrapnel, and died on 4 June from sepsis caused by the horsehair upholstery of his car, which infected his wounds.

ANTHROPOID was to prove controversial because of the appalling civilian reprisals taken by the Nazi occupation forces. All the relatives of the SOE men were rounded up and either executed

or sent to Mauthausen concentration camp. Thousands perished in a wave of executions, and the populations of whole villages were deported to concentration camps. One village, Lidice, was systematically reduced to rubble, the site remaining untouched to this day as a memorial to those who were murdered.

Over 13,000 people suffered arrest in the aftermath of Heydrich's death, prompting many to wonder whether SOE's Czech Section had been wise to launch such a provocative operation. Indeed, there is considerable doubt that SOE did anything more than give logistical support to ANTHROPOID,

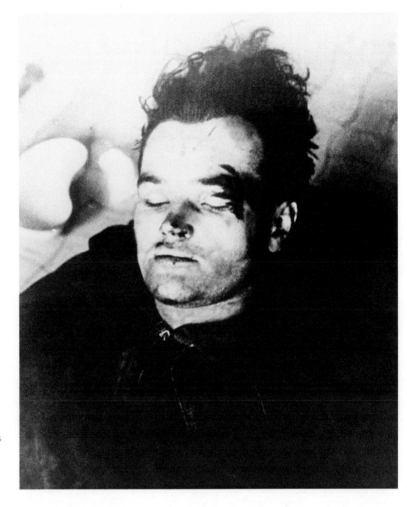

OPPOSITE: The wreckage of Heydrich's car soon after the attack on a Prague street in May 1942.

RIGHT: The body of Jan Kubis after he died in a Prague hospital of wounds sustained during a lengthy gun battle with German troops.

for the plan was certainly Czech in origin, having been hatched by the Czech government-in-exile in London, initially with SS-Gruppenführer Karl Hermann Frank, the Reich-Protektor's hated State Secretary, as the target.

The assassins Kubis and Gabcik, who had transferred to the Free Czech Army from the French Foreign Legion, had been trained by SOE at Arisaig in Scotland and at Bellasis, designated Special Training School 2, and had undergone their parachute course at RAF Ringway, but throughout were still officially attached to the Czech 1st Brigade at Cholmondeley Castle, near Whitchurch in Cheshire. MI6 was also a party to ANTHROPOID, as confirmed by the then head of the Czech Deuxième Bureau, Colonel Frantisek Moravec, who recalled that the scheme "was necessarily shared with several officials of the British MI6, who worked with us on the technical side". Whoever was behind ANTHROPOID, its effect was to decimate the number of potential resisters in Czechoslovakia, reduce the willingness of the inhabitants to help parachutists, and ensure that SOE's Czech Section would play only a peripheral role in the eventual liberation of that country.

21 THE XX COMMITTEE

THE DOUBLE CROSS SYSTEM THAT AIMED
TO CONTROL ALL ENEMY AGENTS IN BRITAIN

CODENAMED TRICYCLE

The XX Committee or Twenty Committee was an inter-departmental committee created on 2 January 1941 to supervise the activity of MI5's growing stable of double agents. Chaired by the Oxford academic John Masterman, with John Marriott acting as its secretary, the committee took its name from the Roman numerals XX – essentially a pun for "double cross" – and met weekly on 227 occasions until 19 May 1945.

Officially a sub-committee of the Wireless Board, the XX Committee included representatives from the Naval Intelligence Division, the director of Military Intelligence, the director of Air Intelligence, the Security Executive, the Secret Intelligence Service (MI6), Home Forces and the Air Ministry branch responsible for the construction of bogus airfields. Also attending were staff from Combined Operations, the Joint Intelligence Committee; the deception planners from Supreme Headquarters Allied Expeditionary Force (SHAEF) Ops (B) and London Controlling Section; the Field Security Police; and the Ministry of Economic Warfare. On average there were about 12 officers at each meeting, held on Thursday afternoons at MI5's headquarters in St James's Street, London. Altogether an estimated 65 officers attended over the committee's lifetime.

In charge of undertaking the XX Committee's ingenious schemes, either submitted by the service departments of the deception planners, or other customers, were MI5's formidable director of counter-espionage, Guy Liddell, and his brilliant subordinate, Tommy Robertson, who led a team of just nine very amiable case officers. Invariably the double agents came to trust their MI5 handlers and lasting friendships were formed among them.

Similar structures were developed in other theatres, such as the 212 Committee, which supervised double agent operations in the 21st Army Group area at SHAEF headquarters. The Thirty Committee operated in Cairo from March 1943 and the Forty Committee supervised activities in Algiers with a representative from the French Deuxième Bureau. In addition, a Fifty Committee worked briefly in Nairobi, and a Sixty Committee oversaw Allied activities in Lisbon.

The incentive behind the XX Committee's creation was MI5's escalating requirement to provide the enemy with information so its double agents could survive, and thrive. By December 1940, with the arrival in London of the Yugoslav Dusan Popov, codenamed TRICYCLE, MI5 had accumulated an impressive number of spies in direct contact with the Abwehr. The pre-war agent SNOW was transmitting meteorological data every morning to Germany from his prison cell in London, and his sub-agent, purportedly a fellow Welsh nationalist and ex-policeman, was submitting written reports to an intermediary in the Spanish embassy. TATE, who had parachuted into Cambridgeshire in September 1940, was in radio contact with the Abwehr in Hamburg. All needed a constant supply of worthwhile, reasonably accurate material to deliver to their controllers who, if they lost interest,

ABOVE: Guy Liddell, MI5's wartime director of counter-espionage and architect of the Double Cross project.

OPPOSITE: Popov's Aliens Registration Act identity card, issued in February 1941, two months after his arrival in London.

LEFT: Dusan Popov, as a young lawyer from Dubrovnik recruited as an Abwehr agent codenamed IVAN.

might be inclined to infiltrate other spies that they considered more reliable.

However, there was the potential for serious conflict with the relevant services unless they were fully indoctrinated into the mysteries of double agent management and were tempted by the advantages of exercising a complete grip on the Axis's sources. MI5 realized that the recruitment of Popov, who was under instructions to build a major spy-ring in London, involving several sub-agents (all MI5 nominees), would transform the somewhat amateurish, desultory approach taken hitherto in the handling of the current agents. This was an opportunity to manipulate aggressively the adversary and, accordingly, MI5 acknowledged the need to compromise strict security by expanding the ring of secrecy regarding double agent operations to include trusted appointees from the military who were sufficiently senior to authorize the disclosure of enough authentic information to make the "chicken feed" more palatable.

The prize was the chance to develop a situation in which the enemy came to rely on individuals whose every act was supervised by skilled MI5 case officers who would draft messages, compare them to details passed on other conduits and make sure to avoid internal contradictions or other slips that an uncoordinated effort might let through. If successful, the advantages were almost unlimited. SNOW's daily wireless traffic, transmitted using a rather primitive hand cipher, was routinely rebroadcast on an Enigma channel, thus allowing cryptanalysts at the RSS in Barnet to monitor the signals and reverse-engineer the daily keys for the Abwehr's machine cipher system.

The biggest challenge for the XX Committee, as it came to realize that all the enemy's agents in Britain were under control, was to engage in a massive deception scheme so as to take the Axis by surprise when the long-expected invasion of Europe took place during the summer of 1944. In accepting conventional military doctrine, the

Abwehr's analysts were pre-disposed to believe that the Allies would land their troops across the shortest route to the beaches in the Pas-de-Calais. This judgement was reinforced by TRICYCLE and TATE, and emphasized by BRUTUS, BRONX and GARBO. By carefully collating the traffic of each double agent to ensure it did not contain any give-away internal contradictions, and by monitoring the enemy's reaction to each message, MI5 supplied the pieces of the intelligence jigsaw puzzle that inevitably led the Axis to over-estimate Allied strengths and conclude that the invaders would cross the Channel from Kent. This sophisticated

ABOVE LEFT: After the war Popov became a successful international businessman and retired to the bishop's palace outside Opio in the south of France.

ABOVE RIGHT: Simone Simon, the French movie actress who had been pursuing a career in Hollywood when she lived with Popov in a New York apartment at 530 Park Avenue.

ABOVE: The Welsh battery manufacturer, Arthur Owens, codenamed SNOW.

deception plan meant that the Normandy landings came as a complete surprise to the German High Command. The Germans were also persuaded to believe that the D-Day assault was a diversionary feint undertaken to draw attention away from the intended objective in northern France.

ABOVE: A German soldier keeps watch on the Atlantic Wall, a series of fortifications intended to protect the Reich from invasion.

ARTHUR OWENS AKA SNOW

Born in April 1899 in Cilybebyll, Arthur Owens was a Welsh inventor and manufacturer of electric accumulators. In 1935 he began supplying Kriegsmarine shipyards in the Baltic with modern batteries for the expanding U-boat fleet. He also reported on his observations of the German shipbuilding programme to the British Admiralty, an assignment he promptly revealed to Nikolaus Ritter of the Hamburg Abwehr.

MI5 detected Owens' duplicity in 1936 when he corresponded with a compromised Abwehr letter-box in Brussels. He was arrested on the first day of the war and detained at Wandsworth prison, where he offered to transmit messages, under MI5's supervision, to his German controller using a suitcase radio he had been given by the Abwehr. This daily broadcast, relayed to Hamburg by a ship cruising off the Norwegian coast, began the Double Cross System. Owens, released from custody and codenamed SNOW, travelled in February 1941 to a rendezvous with Ritter in Lisbon. However, upon his return to London Owens was rearrested and imprisoned, first at Stafford and then at Dartmoor. He was eventually freed in August 1944 and settled in Ireland where he died on Christmas Eve,1957.

Owens' daughter Patricia, who never knew her father's wartime role as a double agent, made a career in Hollywood and starred in the 1958 cult movie *The Fly*.

22. OPERATION NORDPOL

THE ABWEHR'S COUNTER-ESPIONAGE
ENGLANDSPIEL – ENGLAND GAME

THE RADIO GAME

The first attempts by the British SOE's Netherlands (N) Section to infiltrate agents into Nazi-occupied Holland were failures. Its chief, Richard Laming, then parachuted in two agents, Ab Homburg and Corre Sporre, on 6/7 September 1941 to make a short reconnaissance, after which they would be picked up from the coast. The two men were not met at the coast, a mistake which eventually led to the start of a deception by the Germans called NORDPOL that netted them more than 50 Dutch agents.

When the two SOE agents were not met at the coast, they established themselves in Haarlem, where Homburg was recognized and betrayed to the Gestapo on 6 October 1941. He was subsequently sentenced to death but managed to escape from prison the night before his scheduled execution. He eventually made his way back to England by trawler from Ijmuiden, arriving in February 1942 and, after a lengthy debriefing, joined the RAF. Sporre had avoided arrest but when he tried to escape by boat in November he was lost at sea.

A month after Homburg and Sporre had gone missing Laming parachuted in another two agents, Huub Lauwers and Thys Taconis, to look for them. The pair landed safely but their radio proved to be faulty so their first message to London was not transmitted until 3 January 1942. Soon afterwards Taconis traced Homburg and reported his arrest and subsequent escape. London's reply was an instruction that Homburg should make his own way back to England. Lauwers and Taconis then based

themselves in The Hague and maintained a regular radio channel on which they arranged a supply drop on 28 February, which went largely according to plan but Lauwers was arrested a week later, on 6 March, when German direction-finding equipment isolated the address in The Hague. The Germans also recovered his wireless and a quantity of his previous signals. Three days later, Taconis was also taken into custody.

During intensive interrogation Lauwers was persuaded to use his radio to transmit, under German control, back to London. This he did on 12 March, confident that SOE would spot the tell-tale omission of his security check, the procedure of inserting a deliberate mistake at a predetermined position in every message to indicate that the operator was working under duress. Surprisingly, SOE not only acknowledged the signal, but announced the imminent arrival of another agent, Lieutenant Arnold Baatsen. Evidently N Section had failed to spot the absence of the security check in Lauwers's transmission. Baatsen, who had been a professional photographer before the war, duly landed on 27/28 March, marking the start NORDPOL.

In February 1942 Laming had been replaced as the head of SOE's N Section by Charles Blizard, a regular army officer who had himself only been attached to N Section the previous December. The Abwehr's control over Lauwers, Taconis and Baatsen coincided with a dramatic escalation in N Section's activities. The night after Baatsen had

ABOVE: Hermann Giskes, the Abwehr officer who supervised the "radio game" to lure more SOE agents into captivity.

become increasingly desperate following the death of his partner and had been forced to seek help from his friends.

Andringa was coerced into attending a rendezvous on 1 May in a café with Ras, Jordaan and Klooss, but just before the Germans sprang their trap Jordaan slipped away and was able to alert SOE to the arrests. His liberty lasted only a few hours, for both Jordaan and Hendrik Sebes were caught by exploiting information extracted from the others. The Germans then substituted their own operator for Jordaan and re-established contact with SOE, a deception that was only made possible because Jordaan had recently asked for permission to recruit and train his own operator in the field, a highly unusual departure from the standard security procedures. N Section had granted the request, and this message had been discovered among Jordaan's possessions. In this way, the Abwehr was given a second captured radio, which resulted in another parachute operation, on 29 May. This delivered two saboteurs, Antonius van

been dropped, a further two teams followed. The first, which landed safely, consisted of Han Jordaan, a student who had been studying in England, and Gosse Ras, a trader in textiles, but the second pair were not so lucky. Their radio was smashed on impact and Jan Molenaar was mortally injured, leaving his companion, a 28-year-old divinity student, Leonard Andringa, to administer a cyanide capsule to him. Thereafter Andringa made his way to Amsterdam where, devoid of contacts, he lived rough for a while. A third team, of Dunkirk veteran Hendrik Sebes and Barend Klooss, who had recently returned from south-east Asia, followed on 5/6 April and established themselves in Hengelo without incident. The next arrival, on 8/9 April, was Jan De Haas, who was landed by a British torpedo boat with the objective of linking up with Lauwers and Taconis, not realizing both were already in German custody. His search for them failed but on 27 April Lauwers received a fatal message from London instructing him to go to Haarlem to meet De Haas. Instead, the Germans moved in and cornered both De Haas and Andringa, the trainee priest who had

ABOVE: A John Brown-designed B-3 Mark II suitcase radio transceiver of the type widely used by SOE agents operating in enemy-occupied territory.

Steen and Herman Parlevliet, both former Dutch gendarmes, straight into the hands of the enemy and provided the Germans with their third and fourth active wireless links with SOE headquarters.

More were to follow. Jan van Rietschoten, a technical college student who had rowed to England the previous year, and his radio operator Johannes Buizer arrived near Assen on 23/24 June and were forced to send a "safe arrival" signal. A month later Gerard van Hemert dropped straight into an enemy reception committee and was obliged to hand over his radio. When they searched him, the Germans found some orders addressed to Taconis, whom they had imprisoned in March, thus confirming that N Section did not suspect the extraordinary deception game involving six separate wireless channels.

In van Hemert's case the Germans went to elaborate lengths to pretend that Taconis had at least attempted to complete the mission assigned to him by van Hemert – the destruction of a radio station mast at Kootwijk. Allied direction-finding had identified this location as one of the bases used to transmit signals to the U-boat fleet, so it was therefore considered a target of some strategic importance. An assault was planned for 8 August 1942 and Lauwers reported the day afterwards that the attackers had been beaten off by an unexpectedly large number of sentries. This bogus explanation, backed up by a fireworks display at the appropriate moment, satisfied SOE that Taconis had mounted a daring raid. N Section sent its commiserations to Taconis... and announced that he had been decorated with the Military Medal.

The Abwehr nearly achieved a seventh SOE transmitter when a South African, George Dessing, was dropped accidentally into the middle of an SS training camp on 27/28 February 1942. He casually walked out, giving Nazi salutes to the guards, who assumed he was authorized to be there. Later

RIGHT: Abwehr operatives and soldiers encrypting or decrypting messages using Enigma machines.

he had another lucky escape when the Germans tried to use Leo Andringa to entrap him in a café. Sensing that something was wrong, Dessing had casually ambled straight past Andringa's German escort, thereby narrowly avoiding capture for the second time. Realizing that his friend Andringa was under enemy control, Dessing decided to get out of Holland as soon as possible, but he was unable to warn SOE of what had happened because he had no independent means of communication with London. The agent who had been killed on landing, Jan Molenaar, was to have been his radio operator, and without him Dessing was powerless. He did eventually make his way to Switzerland, but he would not reach London until the autumn of 1943.

In the meantime, the duplicity continued and on 26 June 1942 Professor George Jambroes, a senior and influential figure in the Dutch government-in-exile, and his wireless operator Sjef Bukkens, were dropped straight into a German reception committee; Bukkens's radio was used to report on the supposed low morale and security of the Orde Dienst resistance movement in order to undermine British confidence and support for the OD.

On 4/5 September 1942 four more agents followed Jambroes. They were a young student, Knees Drooglever, and an engineer, Karel Beukema. Both were captured, and the former's transmitter became the eighth to join the game. Arie Mooy and Commander Jongelie were next but the latter, a tough naval officer who had worked undercover in the Dutch East Indies, refused to cooperate, so the Germans sent a message to London indicating that he had been fatally injured in the landing. Once again, SOE raised no objection.

At this stage SOE were still clueless. Nine agents were dropped in October and a further four in November. By December 1942 the Germans had captured 43 agents and were controlling 14 different radio channels. In the New Year of 1943 SOE continued to dispatch agents and by April another 13 SOE men had been sent, as well as a woman from MI9, Beatrix Terwindt, whose mission had been to build an escape line. She too was accommodated at the seminary in Haaren, which the Abwehr and Gestapo had acquired to isolate their prisoners. However, the German policy of securing all their captives in the same place led to a leak, which eventually reached the British embassy in Berne in June 1943. For the first time SOE received word that eight British parachutists, including Pieter Dourlein who had arrived on 1/2 March, were in German custody.

Nevertheless, SOE authorized a further operation in May, which sent Anton Mink, Laurens Punt and Oscar de Brey to the cells in Haaren and gave an eighteenth radio link to the Germans. Ingeniously, it was one of these channels that the Abwehr used to smear two of the agents, Dourlein and Johan Ubbink, when they escaped from Haaren on 30 August 1943. Realizing that the entire deception was threatened by this resourceful pair, the Germans reported to SOE that they had actually been captured by the Gestapo and allowed to escape, having been turned. Dourlein and Ubbink eventually reached Berne on 22 November 1943 and gave a detailed account of their experiences. However, both escapees received harsh treatment when they finally reached England, via Gibraltar, on 1 February 1944. They were interrogated at length in London and then moved under open arrest to Guildford. In May they were transferred to Brixton prison, and then released, to be told that one of those who had helped them to escape from Holland, a former police inspector from Tilburg named van Bilsen, had been assassinated by the resistance.

At the end of hostilities much time was spent in determining whether or not, as the Germans had suggested at the time, the information had been supplied to the Abwehr by a traitor within SOE's headquarters in London. The truth was that the Germans were very inventive and devoted considerable resources to exploiting the system over a period of 20 months. It was also an unusual

ABOVE: Flying Officer Ab Homburg (second from right), pictured in September 1944. One of SOE's early agents dropped in Holland. He was captured in 1941 and sentenced to death, but escaped to England where he joined the RAF.

RIGHT: The Englandspiel memorial at Scheveningsebosjes.

example of close coordination between the rival military intelligence services, the Abwehr, and the Gestapo. Both were adept at mounting sophisticated penetration schemes and proved themselves skilled at infiltrating and eliminating other resistance groups. In May 1942, 72 members of the Orde Dienst underground movement were executed, and a further 20 members were shot in July 1943. Survivors were executed at Mauthausen concentration camp in September 1944.

After the war, the principal enemy counter-espionage personnel were brought to London for interrogation and a study was made of captured documents. One in particular made damning reading. The paper listed 46 agents who had been taken prisoner during the operation. Only 17 were described as not having collaborated in any way.

23. CODENAME GARBO

THE DOUBLE AGENT IN THE
D-DAY DECEPTION CAMPAIGN

OPERATION FORTITUDE

Juan Pujol was a Spanish double agent who worked for the Allies. Codenamed GARBO by MI5 and ALARIC by the Abwehr, he submitted false reports from Lisbon to his German handler in Madrid from October 1941. Contacted by MI6, which gave him the codename BOVRIL, Pujol was escorted to London in April 1942 and remained in contact with the Abwehr's Karl-Erich Kühlenthal, by radio and the regular mail, until the end of hostilities.

Supervised by MI5's Tomas Harris, GARBO invented 22 notional sub-agents, including a Dutch airline pilot who supposedly acted as a courier, carrying his messages to Lisbon; an RAF officer assigned to Fighter Command; a Spaniard in the Ministry of Information who obtained a job for GARBO; a left-wing Ministry of Information official; a lovelorn secretary in the War Office; a Portuguese businessman codenamed CARVALHO based in Newport, Monmouthshire, overlooking the Bristol Channel and in touch with Welsh nationalists; William Gerbers, a married Swiss businessman in Bootle who died of cancer in October 1942; William Gerbers's widow; a wealthy Venezuelan student, codenamed BENEDICT, who acted as ALARIC's deputy and had a brother in Canada, codenamed MOONBEAM; a non-commissioned RAF officer; a lieutenant in the British 49th Division; a Greek Communist seaman who deserted from the merchant navy and believed he was working for the Soviets; a Gibraltarian waiter codenamed FRED who worked in a storage depot in the Chislehurst

REPÚBLICA DOS ESTADOS UNIDOS DO BRASIL
FICHA CONSULAR DE QUALIFICAÇÃO
MODÊLO S.C. 139

Esta ficha, expedida em duas vias, será entregue à Polícia Marítima e à Imigração no pôrto de destino

Nome por extenso Juan Pujol Garcia
Admitido em território nacional em caráter Temporário (temporário ou permanente)
Nos termos do art. 25 letra A do dec. n. 3.010, de 1938
Lugar e data de nascimento Barcelona em 14/2/1912
Nacionalidade Espanhola Estado civil casado
Filiação (nome do Pai e da Mãe) Juan Pujol Pena e de Mercedes Garcia Guijarro Profissão Escritor
Residência no país de origem Rua Nueva nº 26, Lugo-Espanha.

NOME	IDADE	SEXO
Juan Fernando	mezes	Masculino

FILHOS MENORES DE 18 ANOS

Passaporte n. 892 expedido pelas autoridades de Consulado de Espanha em Lisboa na data 12/9/1940
sado sob n.

ASSINATURA DO PORTADOR:

NOTA—Esta ficha deve ser preenchida à máquina pela autoridade consular, sendo as duas vias em original.

Consulado Geral do Brasil em Lisboa
de de 19 41
O CÔNSUL GERAL:

LEFT: Juan Pujol's registration card issued by the Brazilian Consulate in Lisbon in 1941.

OPPOSITE: GARBO's message of condolence sent to his Abwehr controller in Madrid upon the news of Hitler's death.

G A R B O

Tuesday 8th May 1945

Message sent 1919 hours GMT

SPANISH

Gr 55

LA NOTICIA DE LA MUERTE DE NUESTRO QUERIDO JEFE SOBREPASA
LOS LIMITES DE NUESTRA PROFUNDA FE EN EL DESTINO QUE LE
ESPERA A NUESTRA POBRE EUROPA PERO SUS HECHOS Y LA HISTORIA
DE SU INMOLACION POR QUERER SALVAR AL MUNDO DEL PELIGRO
DE ANARQUIA QUE LE AMENAZA PERDURARA SIEMPRE EN EL CORAZON
DE TODO HOMBRE DE BUENA VOLUNTAD X

ENGLISH TRANSLATION

News of the death of our dear Chief shocks our profound faith

in the destiny which awaits our poor Europe, but his deeds and

the story of his sacrifice to save the world from the danger of

anarchy which threatens us will last for ever in the hearts of

all men of goodwill.

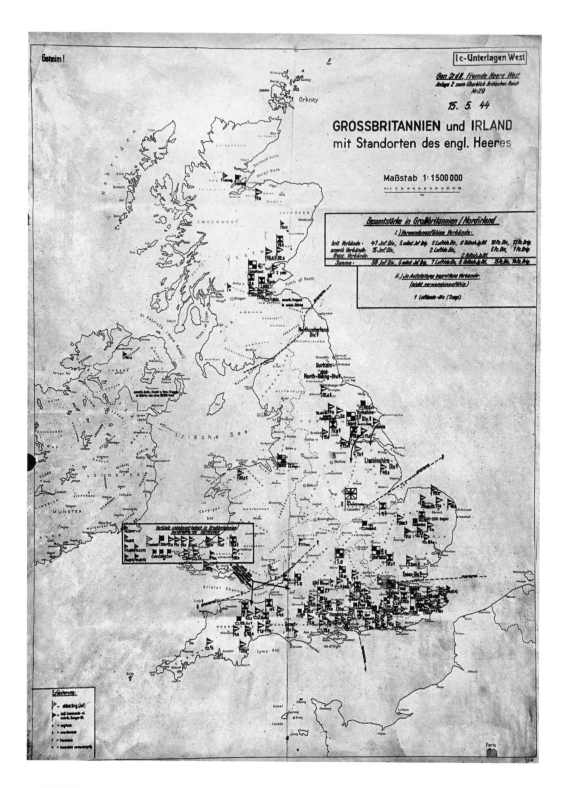

OPPOSITE: A German map dated 15 May 1944 captured in Italy showing the latest assessment of Allied forces in Great Britain, including the bogus units reported by GARBO.

RIGHT: Juan Pujol's photograph, which was on his British identity card.

caves; a Spanish republican codenamed ALMURA who worked as ALARIC's radio operator; a guard in the Chislehurst munitions depot, recruited by FRED; MOONBEAM's cousin, codenamed CON; a Welsh nationalist seaman from Swansea, known as Stanley and codenamed DAGOBERT; a soldier in the British 9th Armoured Division who supplied information to DAGOBERT; a retired seaman named David, living in Dover and leading the World Aryan Order, codenamed DONNY; Theresa Jardine, a member of the Women's Royal Naval Service codenamed GLEAM; a cousin of DONNY's living in Swansea; and the treasurer of the World Aryan Order, living in Harwich and codenamed DORICK.

Although most of GARBO's spy-ring were imaginary, one in particular was semi-authentic. Codenamed DICK, he sent letters in his distinctive handwriting to the Abwehr in Madrid. He was Pilot Officer Martin Grimaldi, the Field Security Police officer attached to MI5's B1(b) sub-section who had masqueraded as SIX, posing as a South African posted to Algiers as a linguist soon after the TORCH landings in Algeria, and was virulently anti-Communist. Known as DICK, his distinctive handwriting had become familiar to his German controller in Madrid, so when he was killed on 3 July 1943 in an air accident flying from Tiree to RAF Machrihanish in the Outer Hebrides at the end of his week's leave in June, a similar excuse was found for his alleged demise in North Africa. The youngest of four brothers, sons of a vicar in east Devon who all joined the RAF, Martin Grimaldi had transferred to MI5 on the recommendation of a family friend, Charles Cholmondeley, a B Division

REPÚBLICA DOS ESTADOS UNIDOS DO BRASIL

MODÊLO S.C. 139

FICHA CONSULAR DE QUALIFICAÇÃO

Esta ficha, expedida em duas vias, será entregue à Policia Maritima e à Imigração no pôrto de destino

Nome por extenso Araceli Gonzalez de Pujol

Admitido em território nacional em caráter Temporário
(temporário ou permanente)

Nos termos do art. 25 letra A do dec. n. 3.010 , de 1938

Lugar e data de nascimento Lugo em 5 / 7 / 1919

Nacionalidade Espanhola Estado civil casada

Filiação (nome do Pai e da Mãe) Salvador Gonzalez Carbalho e
Margarita Gonzalez Perez Profissão Não tem

Residência no país de origem Rua Nueva nº 26, Lugo-Espanha.

NOME   IDADE   SEXO

FILHOS
MENORES
DE 18 ANOS

Passaporte n. 892 expedido pelas autoridades de Consulado de
Espanha em Lisboa na data 12/9/1940

sado sob n.

ASSINATURA DO PORTADOR:

NOTA—Esta ficha deve ser preenchida à máquina pela autoridade consular, tendo a duas vias ao original.

SÊLO
CON

Consulado Geral do Brasil
em Lisboa

de de 19 41

O CÔNSUL GERAL:

LEFT: The Brazilian Consulate registration for GARBO's wife Araceli Pujol.

OPPOSITE: The German High Command assessment issued days after D-Day predicting the imminent attack in the Pas-de-Calais, causing the cancellation of a planned armoured counter-attack in Normandy.

officer. He had spent his leave with his eldest brother, Dr C.E. Grimaldi, who was serving as a medical officer on Tiree, but his plane, a Fokker XXII, had experienced an engine fire and killed the crew of five and all 20 passengers.

DICK's first letter containing secret writing, supposedly posted from Algiers to Lisbon in January 1943 and had been well received, even though the content had taken six weeks to reach its destination. This very convenient time lapse had been exploited by MI5 to make it appear that at the time of its composition the letter had included some high-level, accurate information. Supposedly ten such letters had been mailed to GARBO's bank in London, where he had deleted various incriminating items, such as the signature, addressee and the name of the Field Censorship official who had approved the innocuous content. Then GARBO inserted the letter in the binding of a book, which had been passed to a seaman courier for posting in Lisbon to an Abwehr cover address in Madrid. In reality, the letter had been fabricated in London and then delivered in the MI6 bag to Portugal, where the package was placed in the mail on a date that coincided with the arrival of a ship from England, thereby supporting the false narrative.

In July 1943 GARBO reported that DICK's mistress, Dorothy, had informed him that her lover had been killed in an air crash while travelling to his new posting. All his kit had also been destroyed, eliminating the risk that his supply of secret ink might have been discovered among his belongings. Both MI5 and the Abwehr closed their files on DICK.

GARBO participated in numerous deception schemes, including the principal role in Operation FORTITUDE, the deception operation to mislead Germany before the Normandy landings. He continued to operate undetected until the end of hostilities, and he visited Kühlenthal in Spain to be paid off. Altogether GARBO received in excess of £40,000 from the Abwehr, which paid for much of MI5's wartime cost.

After the war Pujol moved with his wife and two sons to Venezuela where he worked as a language teacher for Shell Oil at the Maracaibo refinery. He later ran a hotel and his wife Araceli had a third child, Maria. However, Araceli was homesick for Spain and arranged to return to Madrid with the children. Juan agreed, and promised to follow her once he had sold their house and car. Instead he remained in Caracas and persuaded MI6 to report his death to his wife in Spain.

Unaware that her husband had faked his own death, Araceli subsequently married an American diplomat who retired to open one of Madrid's most successful art galleries. Meanwhile, Juan also married again, and had two further sons.

Neither family was aware of the other until June 1984 when, on the 40th anniversary of the D-Day landings, Juan was invited to Buckingham Palace to receive the decoration he had been awarded in conditions of great secrecy during the war. With his cover finally blown, and the exploits of GARBO revealed for the first time, Juan was reunited with the children of his first marriage.

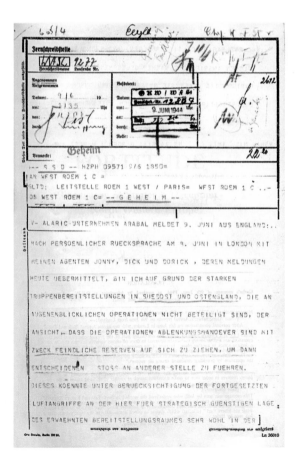

FORTITUDE

FORTITUDE proved to be GARBO's greatest triumph, and evidence emerged after the war of the scheme's efficacy. The deception campaign, undertaken in 1944, was intended to persuade the Nazis that the invasion of France would take place in the Pas-de-Calais. The objective was to protect Operation OVERLORD, the D-Day landings in Normandy. The plan included the creation of a fictitious military force, the First United States Army Group (FUSAG), which appeared to generate wireless traffic indicating a concentration of its component units in East Anglia. Bogus radio transmissions, false reports from double agents and the construction of dummy planes and landing craft combined to enhance the impression conveyed to the enemy that FUSAG, commanded by General George Patton, would embark in south-east England for the Pas-de-Calais some weeks after an initial feint had diverted German troops to Normandy. Captured intelligence indicated that the Germans accepted FUSAG as genuine and overestimated Allied strength.

Many of the agent observations were made by BRUTUS, and TATE, but as the invasion neared, the burden of conveying the skilfully fabricated information fell on GARBO because TATE's performance could not be completely monitored, and BRUTUS's alleged position as a Polish liaison officer at FUSAG headquarters made him too dangerous.

24. CODENAME MAX AND MORITZ

KONSPIRATSIA: SOVIET DECEPTION OPERATIONS

ON THE RUSSIAN FRONT

THE KLATT CONUNDRUM

In early 1942 the British RSS began monitoring the wireless traffic of an Abwehr source located in Eastern Europe. Codenamed MORITZ, the source was supplying information that appeared to originate on the Sofia to Vienna Enigma channel with the callsigns SCHWERT and VERA, relaying messages from the Middle East. Between December 1941 and March 1942 40 messages from MORITZ were read, and in August 1942 MI6's Section V reviewed the texts and, having rejected the possibility that they were based on signals intelligence, judged them to have "a professional flavour, being up to date, terse, well-arranged and definite", noting that the information came from "Syria through Iraq and Persia to Egypt and Libya" but concluding that "there were no clues to the sources of the MORITZ reports". The content varied in quality from patently false to uncannily accurate. During the period of interception, in 1942 and 1943, almost 1,000 messages were intercepted and decrypted.

The most striking feature of the MORITZ reports was that they were detailed yet, for the most part, so inaccurate that could be explained either as a deliberate attempt to deceive the Germans or as a concoction put out for mercenary reasons. The resulting analysis concluded that a transmitter in the Spanish embassy in Ankara, codenamed ANKER, was in daily contact with SCHWERT, the Abwehrstelle in Sofia, using a hand cipher. The exact same messages were then relayed from Sofia to VERA in Vienna on an Enigma channel at the same time each afternoon, except Sundays. Each of the transmissions consisted of four or five messages from another network called MAX, and just one or two from MORITZ. VERA, the Vienna Abwehrstelle headed by the Graf Rudolf von Marogna-Redwitz, then passed the messages on to BURG, the Abwehr's headquarters in Berlin. Within half an hour, BURG was circulating the reports to Fremde Heere Ost at the Boyen Fortress in Lotzen, eastern Prussia, and to the High Command headquarters in Rome. The circuit opened in October 1940 and broadcast a final signal on 13 February 1945.

RIGHT: The Oxford academic Gilbert Ryle. He was one of the Radio Security Service cryptographers who undertook a study of Abwehr signals traffic in eastern Europe, centred in Sofia, to determine the identify and loyalty of a supposedly well-informed spy-ring apparently operating behind the Soviet lines.

OPPOSITE: The Abwehr spy, codenamed KLATT, who masterminded the MAX and MORITZ signals traffic on the Russian front that baffled British intercept operators.

A lengthy study of the traffic conducted by the RSS revealed that MAX and MORITZ were part of an Abwehr department headed by a certain Fritz Klatt, a name that turned out to be an alias adopted by a Czech Jew, Richard Kauder, whose network of more than 70 agents, of whom around a dozen were Jews, accounted for much of the Sofia station's activities. Kauder operated from a firm that he owned, the Mittermeyer Import-Export Company, based at 55 Skoolev Street, not far from Otto Wagner's War Ministry at 57 Patriarch Aphtimey Street in Sofia.

The RSS study, conducted by Gilbert Ryle, posed a series of questions. How could Klatt's network submit reports from Cairo to Sofia on the same day? Some of the messages referred to events that had taken place across the Middle East the previous day. One significant characteristic of the traffic was the frequent misspellings of names, and the use of Russian names, for example Galiopolia for Heliopolis. Similarly, fighter aircraft were described as *isterbaitle*.

Broadly, the information from the Middle East did not pose a serious threat to the Allies, and much of it could have been gleaned by the Germans from other sources. The reporting was long on generalities but short on specifics, but the decision was taken to inform the Soviets of the existence of MAX and MORITZ. The news was delivered at a meeting convened with Josef Stalin in Moscow by the MI6 representative, Cecil Barclay, on 19 April 1943, in the presence of the ambassador, Archie Clark Kerr. Curiously, the Soviets seemed uninterested, despite a further conference with the director of Military Intelligence, General Fyodor Kuznetsov, on 29 July, and the traffic continued, apparently unaffected, so the British concluded that the entire organization was operating under the supervision of Soviet military intelligence, the NKVD and therefore was part of some elaborate deception campaign.

That verdict had been reached after the most intensive scrutiny conducted by both MI5 and

ABOVE: Gilbert Ryle, the wartime cryptographer who made a special study of the Abwehr radio traffic along the Russian front.

Section V, which included a veracity check on 49 messages decrypted in June and July 1943, of which only five were thought to have any value. Thirty-three were shown to be useless, and 11 could not be subjected to any comparison.

Research into MAX and MORITZ escalated after the war when captured Abwehr officers underwent interrogation by the Allies in an effort to identify the organization's sources. MAX turned out to be General Anton Turkul, a Ukrainian who had fought against the Bolsheviks in the Russian Civil War with the whites and had later settled in comfortable exile in Paris. When interviewed, Turkul revealed that the codenames MAX and MORTITZ were not individual agents, but codenames for groups of geographically based networks, MAX being Ukraine and Russia, and MORITZ being Turkey and the Middle East. He alleged that the names had been inspired by Wilhelm Busch's illustrated rhyming tales, *Max and Moritz: A Story of Seven Boyish Pranks*, published in 1865, and admitted that he had worked for the NKVD for years, and that Kauder had quickly realized that his own organization was actually sponsored by the Soviets.

Kauder, who was arrested by the Gestapo in February 1945, was freed from prison in Vienna by American troops in May 1945 and under interrogation he admitted that his entire organization had been run by the NKVD, but he had decided, for reasons of self-preservation (because he was already in fear of the Gestapo), not to tell the Abwehr. He was later transferred to Camp King in Oberrursel where he was questioned by Klop Ustinov, and then in 1946 by Gilbert Ryle.

Kauder's candour helped explain MAX and MORITZ and provided eloquent proof that the NKVD was ruthless enough to accept hideous sacrifices to enhance the status of a valued double agent. This was classic spy tradecraft, conforming to the principles of *konspiratsia*, in which deception, or *maskirova*, is an objective and not merely a technique. Evidently, the Abwehr had been duped by

ABOVE: General Anton Turkul, the White Russian who pretended to his Abwehr controllers that he ran an extensive network of agents across eastern Europe.

signals originating on the Russian Front purporting to be the transmissions of a German spy operating behind the Soviet lines. According to RSS analysts, the MAX traffic originated from areas along the line from Leningrad to Rostov and Kerch through the Caucasus from the north; from Novosibirsk to Batumi from Georgia, Azerbaijan and Armenia; from Iran, Baghdad and Basra as well as Kuibyshev and Astrakhan; and from the western side of the Caspian Sea. The authenticity of much of the material, and the huge losses consequently suffered by the Red Army, were factors in persuading the Germans to accept the information as genuine.

The MAX traffic proved to be one of the enduring mysteries of Second World War. It was never clear if MAX was a double agent working under the control of the NKVD. During the post-war quadripartite occupation of Vienna, Kauder was abducted by the NKVD. His fate and loyalties remain a conundrum.

25. OPERATION DRAGOON

THE MARCH TO VE-DAY

UNDERCOVER AGENT PAULINE

Operation DRAGOON was the name given to the Allied planned invasion of the south of France in August 1944. Unlike the D-Day landings three months earlier, DRAGOON was heavily reliant on French Resistance *maquisards*, who engaged the enemy and seized the route from Cannes to Grenoble to assist the US 7th Army's break-out from the coast.

One of the lessons learned from D-Day's Operation OVERLORD was the advantage of deploying irregular paramilitaries to harass the enemy and prevent reinforcements destined for the front lines from reaching their destination. The adoption of unorthodox tactics had proved very effective, for example in delaying the 2nd SS Panzer Division *Das Reich* as it tried to move north from Toulouse to launch a counter-attack on the invaders. The route, which should have been completed in 72 hours, took 17 days. Another was the preference to engage in hit-and-run guerrilla raids and the need to avoid pitched battles against superior forces.

Accordingly, the British SOE would play a major role in DRAGOON, and in November 1943 the successful head of the JOCKEY circuit, Francis Cammaerts, was recalled to London to be briefed on his next mission, into southern France, landing near Seyne in Haute Provence in February 1944. A former schoolmaster and conscientious objector, Cammaerts had been flown into northern France in March 1943 to run an operation called DONKEYMAN, but the network had been betrayed, forcing him to move to the Haute Savoie.

By the time General Alexander Patch's 100,000

troops landed on the beaches of St Tropez unopposed in mid-August 1944, Cammaerts was exercising command over more than 10,000 *résistants* in the Vercors. When the German army attempted to surround them at least two divisions were diverted to the task. Although this was not a deliberate strategy pre-planned by Allied headquarters, it had the merit of tying up the enemy's hard-stretched resources at a critical moment.

Accompanied by two other SOE agents, Cammaerts was arrested by the local paramilitary (the *Milice*), which supported the occupying forces, in a routine checkpoint just two days before DRAGOON was scheduled to begin. They were detained in

OPPOSITE: Christine Granville.

RIGHT: DRAGOON becomes front-page news worldwide.

OVERLEAF: The U.S. 3rd Infantry Division lands at Cavalaire, the most westerly of the three French beaches selected for the Allied invasion of the South of France. The landings were largely unopposed.

Digne, where the trio underwent interrogation at the notorious Villa Marie-Louise and were condemned to death, with the execution set for the evening of 17 August 1944. Although the SS intelligence agency had circulated a regional alert for Cammaerts, known by his *nom de guerre* "Roger", his inquisitors never realized his true identity.

One of Cammaerts's subordinates was Christine Granville, née the Countess Krystyna Skarbek, a fiery Polish adventuress who had worked for MI6 in

Belgrade before joining SOE. She was operating for SOE in France using the codename Pauline. Most recently, she had been instrumental in persuading an entire battalion of Polish garrison troops near the frontier at Col-de-Larche to desert the Germans and join the partisans.

Determined to rescue Cammaerts, she obtained an interview with the Gestapo in Digne and claimed to be Cammaerts's wife... and the niece of Field Marshal Montgomery. She persuaded a

ABOVE: U.S. troops land on the beaches in the south of France unopposed during operation DRAGOON.

OPPOSITE: Barrage balloons protect the embarkation of troops at Nisida, north of Naples, in anticipation of DRAGOON.

member of the local *Milice*, Albert Schenck, to cooperate, and he put her in touch with a Belgian interpreter employed by the Gestapo, Max Waem, who negotiated a bribe of two million francs. Both men were threatened with instant arrest after the liberation, which seemed imminent, and Granville transmitted a message to London requesting the ransom money, which was delivered by parachute from SOE's base in Algiers 48 hours later.

Moments before the scheduled execution, Cammaerts and his two SOE companions, Xan Fielding and Christian Sorensen, were escorted by Schenck and Waem to a car and driven to a rendezvous with Granville before returning to Seyne. SOE honoured Granville's promise to free Schenck, who was promptly murdered by the Free French, but Waem, with a rather more sinister reputation, is thought to have survived the war, having offered his services as a spy for the Allies.

DRAGOON proved a great Allied success, liberating southern France in just four weeks and quickly capturing the important Mediterranean ports of Toulon and Marseilles. The German Army Group G was forced to withdraw north, first to Dijon and then to the Vosges mountains, having suffered heavy losses.

Both Cammaerts and Granville were decorated in London and Paris for their extraordinary gallantry. After the war Cammaerts returned to teaching and was appointed headmaster of Alleyne's School in Stevenage. He retired to the south of France in 1987 and died in 2006. Christine Granville was not financially rewarded for her efforts during the war. She found a job as a stewardess on the Union-Castle Line, a British shipping company, and was stabbed to death by a spurned lover in a Kensington hotel in June 1952. Her murderer, Dennis Muldowney, was hanged at Pentonville in September 1952.

26. THE ROTE KAPELLE NETWORK

SOVIET ESPIONAGE IN THE REICH

GRU NETWORKS

The name Rote Kapelle (Red Orchestra or Red Chapel) was the name given to a Soviet intelligence agency (GRU) network in Brussels. It was uncovered by the Abwehr in 1941 when it was headed by Leopold Trepper, an experienced GRU officer who had lived in France and Palestine before building a network in Western Europe.

On the night of 12/13 December 1941 the Abwehr, guided by radio direction-finders, raided 101 rue des Atrebates in the Etterbeek district of Brussels and arrested an illicit wireless operator who gave his name as de Smets. In fact he was Lieutenant Anton Danilov of the GRU who had been posted to Paris as an assistant military attaché in 1938 and subsequently had been transferred to Vichy. In mid-1941 he had moved to Brussels to work for Viktor Guryevitch as a communications expert.

Danilov had been transmitting when the Germans burst into the house early in the morning and, in a fierce struggle, he was overcome. A few hours later, his controller, Trepper, who happened to be visiting Brussels, called at the house and was questioned by the Germans, but he was sufficiently well equipped with authentic papers to bluff his way out of a potentially very awkward situation. Alerted to Danilov's arrest, Trepper succeeded in warning his principal sub-agent, Viktor Guryevitch, of what

BELOW: The Sonderkommando assigned the task of investigating the GRU's spy-ring based in Brussels and Berlin.

RIGHT: Harro Schulze-Boysen, the anti-Nazi Luftwaffe officer and Soviet spy codenamed CORPORAL who was arrested in August 1942 and hanged four months later.

had happened, and he promptly fled to Paris, but another contact, Mikhail Makarov, was not so lucky. He also called at the house on the day of Danilov's arrest and was taken into custody.

Once the Germans had solved the ciphers, they were able to backtrack, and the Abwehr's chief cryptographer, Dr Wilhelm Vauck, succeeded in decrypting around 200 of the Rote Kapelle's signals that had been intercepted and recorded. On 15 July 1942, Vauck tackled a message from "the DIREKTOR, Moscow", dated 10 October 1941

and addressed to a certain KENT, one of several texts that disclosed three addresses belonging to the network. Accordingly, the occupants of those three places were placed under surveillance and identified as Harro Schulze-Boysen of the Air Ministry; Arvid Harnack, a respected academic; and Adam Kuckhoff, a film producer. Another of these compromising messages decoded by Vauck referred to Saalestrasse 36, the Berlin address of a young woman allegedly named Ilse who was also of some importance. A further message, dated

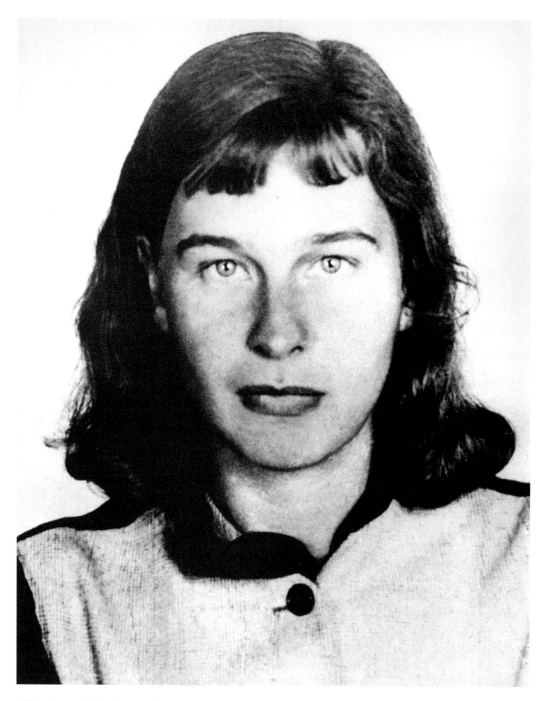

ABOVE: Libertas Shulze-Boysen, a former member of the
Nazi party who became a Soviey spy and was executed with
her husband in Berlin in December 1942.

28 August 1941 and decrypted retrospectively, made it clear that Ilse was her true name.

Gestapo inquiries showed Ilse Stöbe to be working for Theodor Wolff at the Reich Foreign Ministry, and that before the war she had been a correspondent for various Swiss newspapers. She was arrested in Hamburg, and under interrogation she revealed that she had been the mistress of Rudolf Herrnstadt, a notorious *Berliner Tageblatt* journalist who had defected to Moscow in 1933. Despite the seniority and sensitivity of her post, Stöbe had kept in touch with Herrnstadt, who became a senior GRU officer supervising clandestine air drops into Germany and had even allowed Ilse's address to be given to GRU parachutists for use as a safe-house. Before her execution on 22 December 1942, Stöbe implicated Schulze-Boysen, Harnack, and Rudolf von Scheliha, a diplomat in the Foreign Ministry's information section. Once Stöbe had named the three, their entire network amounting to 80 sub-agents was rounded up and either hanged or beheaded.

A subsequent Reich security agency investigation concluded that Harnack and Schulze-Boysen, both Communist activists for many years, had been recruited by the GRU quite recently, in 1941. They had been given a wireless transmitter by Alexander Erdberg of the Soviet Trade Delegation in Berlin before its withdrawal in June 1941, but they never achieved direct contact with Moscow as intended.

In August 1941, Guryevitch had given them another set, but again they failed to establish direct contact and instead had relied upon couriers to pass messages to the Soviet embassy in Stockholm and to Johann Wenzel in Brussels. This development led inevitably to the arrest of Wenzel, a German Communist from Danzig who had been trained as a radio operator in Moscow, and the capture of his ciphers.

The quality of the information reaching Moscow from Berlin was unprecedented, for among the members of the ring were Herbert Gollnow, an Abwehr liaison officer at the headquarters of the High Command of the armed forces responsible for supervising clandestine air operations on the Russian Front; Lieutenant Wolfgang Havemann of the navy's intelligence branch; and Horst Heilmann, an Abwehr cryptographer who was having an affair with Schulze-Boysen's wife, Libertas. All were interrogated and then hanged at Ploetzensee prison.

Rudolf von Scheliha, a more experienced Soviet agent, suffered the same fate. He had been recruited while serving at the German embassy in Warsaw in 1934 and had been paid for his information through a Swiss bank. As well as being compromised by Stöbe, he was incriminated by Heinrich Koenen, a German Communist who had parachuted into Osterode in eastern Prussia in October 1942 with instructions to contact Stöbe. By the time he landed, she was already in the hands of the Gestapo, and when he was arrested on 22 October, he was found to be carrying a receipt confirming a transfer of $7,500 to von Scheliha's bank account.

The Rote Kapelle's commercial front, Simex, survived the German occupation until November 1942, when raids were mounted simultaneously in both Brussels and Paris. The companies had fallen under suspicion soon after the arrest of Konstantin Efremov, an experienced GRU officer and chemical warfare expert who had been operating in Western Europe under student cover since about 1936. Under pressure, the Ukrainian had agreed to cooperate with the Abwehr and divulged enough information to compromise Simex in Paris, which led them to Trepper.

When caught, Trepper volunteered to cooperate with the Germans, apparently motivated by the very justifiable fear that the Soviets would execute his entire family if they learned of his arrest. Not only did Trepper betray Henry Robinson, Léo Grossvogel, Isidore Springer and other members of the network, but he also agreed to transmit to Moscow as a double agent. While the SS intelligence agency, the Sicherheitsdienst (SD), negotiated with Trepper, elaborate precautions were taken to prevent the news of his arrest from leaking.

Trepper's capture came only a fortnight after the arrest in Marseilles of Guryevitch and his mistress, Margarete Barcza. Unwisely, Guryevitch had opened a branch of Simex in Marseilles after he had fled from Belgium following the arrests there, and once Efremov had started to help the enemy, the Simex cover was utterly compromised. Guryevitch was escorted to Berlin for interrogation, where he admitted his GRU codename KENT, and in March 1943 agreed to transmit to Moscow from Paris as MARS, under the SD's control. By Christmas 1942, the Germans had unravelled an extraordinary series of interlocking networks and taken control of most of the senior Soviet personnel. Trepper seemed entirely cooperative and initiated a wireless link with Moscow codenamed EIFFEL. He ensured Robinson's arrest and arranged for the entrapment of Grossvogel, together with three others, at the Café de la Paix in Paris. He also denounced Isadore Springer and thereby betrayed an entire independent ring based in Lyons.

Through Trepper the Germans were able to recover the famous Robinson Papers, an archive of Soviet illegal activity in Europe dating back to the 1920s. When Robinson was arrested in December 1942, a search of his hotel room revealed a briefcase hidden under the floorboards, full of documents, forged identity papers and texts of messages. Among the many branches of the GRU compromised by Robinson was an important wireless transmitter run by Dr Hersog Sokol for the French Communist Party at his home in Le Rancy, through which Trepper had relayed messages to Moscow via London. Although Polish in origin, Sokol was a physician prominent in the Belgian Communist Party. He and his wife Mariam were arrested on 9 June 1942 and both later died in captivity.

ABOVE: Luba Trepper, wife of the Rote Kapelle's chief, Leopold Trepper, who was captured by the Germans and pretended to cooperate so he could escape. She campaigned for his post-war release from Poland.

As well as scrutinizing the Robinson Papers and obtaining Trepper's apparently enthusiastic assistance, the Germans also persuaded Efremov to change sides and work as a double agent. With a prominent Dutch Communist, Winterink Efremov, and EIFFEL in radio contact with Moscow, and Guryevitch promising to cooperate, the Germans believed they had taken control of much of the GRU's illegal networks in France, Belgium and the Netherlands, and had eliminated the organization's entire branch in Germany, but in fact Trepper had succeeded both in winning the confidence of the Germans, who thought he had genuinely switched sides, and also in alerting Moscow Centre to his arrest. Similarly, Johann Wenzel eluded his German captors in November 1942 and sent a message to the Soviet embassy in London that Efremov was in enemy hands and that his radio was operating under control.

Although Trepper appears to have betrayed a large number of his subordinates to the enemy, he kept a single contact at liberty and used this line of communication to keep Moscow informed of developments. The GRU responded by protecting their star agent and participating in a complicated triple game of wireless deception, a *funkspiel* that may have been part of a sophisticated contingency plan but certainly one that was maintained until Trepper's escape from German captivity in September 1943.

Trepper was later to insist that his escape had been prompted by his discovery that the Abwehr had closed down a previously unknown transmitter run by the French Communist Party near Lyons and recovered a large quantity of back-traffic that was to be scrutinized by Vauck. Fearing that the Sonderkommando was on the point of learning how he had duped his captors, Trepper eluded his escort while under guard in the centre of Paris and went into hiding for the rest of the war. Intriguingly, Trepper wrote four letters to Vauck's Sonderkommando, in which he pretended to have been abducted and reassured the SD that Moscow remained ignorant of the *funkspiel*. Notwithstanding Trepper's escape, and despite the Abwehr's confidence that the Rote Kapelle had been eliminated, the network continued to function, albeit under German supervision.

Altogether an estimated 217 arrests were made in connection with the Rote Kapelle investigation, of whom 143 committed suicide, died in captivity or were executed.

A post-war study of the Robinson Papers revealed the existence of a hitherto unsuspected British branch of the Rote Kapelle headed by a concert pianist, Ernest D. Wiess, who agreed to cooperate with MI5. Born in Breslau in 1902, Weiss had been recruited into the GRU by a former university contemporary and had agreed to travel to England on a long-term mission. He arrived on 11 May 1932 and was supervised by an illegal support officer codenamed HARRY I who arranged for him to meet two seamen who subsequently

ABOVE: Arvid Harnack, a respected university lecturer arrested by the Gestapo with 80 co-conspirators, and executed for espionage.

acted as his couriers. In 1935 Weiss travelled to Enge in Switzerland to meet his new controller, HARRY II. This meeting resulted in Weiss handling British secrets stolen by two Soviet agents, an Air Ministry official named Major Wilfred Vernon and an Irishman, Frederick Meredith. Both were overt members of the CPGB working at the Royal Aircraft Establishment at Farnborough who had visited Russia in a group of eight tourists in May 1932. Weiss, who had by now adopted the identity of "Walter Lock", ran Vernon and Meredith until August 1937 when, during his absence on holiday, Vernon's home was ransacked by burglars. In the subsequent police investigation Vernon was found to have accumulated a quantity of classified documents, and this led to his prosecution and dismissal in October on a charge of unauthorized possession of government documents. He was elected the Labour MP for Dulwich in 1945.

27. OPERATION GREIF

OTTO SKORZENY'S COMMANDOS IN
THE BATTLE OF THE BULGE

A SWASHBUCKLING ADVENTURER

During the surprise German offensive the Battle of the Bulge in the Ardennes in December 1944, commandos trained by the legendary SS officer Otto Skorzeny were deployed behind the Allied lines to seize vital bridges across the river Meuse at Arnay, Huy and Ardenne before they could be destroyed by the Allies. The plan, devised by Hitler, was designed to wreak havoc by disrupting communications and creating confusion among the retreating troops so they would be unable to reform and develop defensive positions. The key element in the anticipated success of this operation was Skorzeny's controversial decision to dress his infiltrating troops in captured enemy uniforms.

This strategy did not take the Allies entirely by surprise, in that there had been rumours for some months that the Germans had been collecting uniforms from prisoner-of-war camps. This had been reported to Winston Churchill by MI5 in March 1944. Then, in the weeks before and after the D-Day landings, evidence developed, mainly from signal interceptions, of elaborate preparations for stay-behind networks in areas likely to be liberated by the Allies. Finally, there was a strong expectation, developed mainly from prisoner interrogations, that the Nazis had plans for an extensive organization, known as Werewolf, which would conduct guerrilla resistance operations after an Allied occupation of the Reich.

The plan, codenamed GREIF (Griffin), was to assemble a brigade-strength force of English-speaking volunteers, equipped with captured

enemy vehicles and weapons, at the SS barracks in Neustrelitz, Mecklenburg, so they could train for the "false flag" mission. The individual teams would include demolition squads, sabotage units and assault groups, but in the event a severe lack of suitable personnel and equipment dictated a significant reduction in the scale of the plan.

Skorzeny's men, designated Panzerbrigade 10,

were brought to Bad Munstereifel for the beginning of the offensive, and dispersed among the three participating armoured divisions, the 1st SS Panzer, the 12th SS Panzer and the 12th Volksgrenadiers. However, when the battle began, few of the initial objectives were taken, and the commandos were reassigned to the attack on Malmedy, which was repelled by the American defenders.

Another component of GREIF was to be a simultaneous attack on SHAEF at Paris, where the intention was to assassinate the Supreme Commander, General Dwight D. Eisenhower. The SD had recruited a group of *Jagdverband* for the task of parachuting into the area and then bluffing

OPPOSITE: Otto Skorzeny, the Vienna-born SS officer who undertook a series of daring high-risk operations at Hitler's personal request.

BELOW: The execution of three GREIF commandos on 23 December 1944.

their way into the headquarters, but that part of the operation was compromised when three German commandos, Manfred Pernass, Günther Billing and Wilhelm Schmidt, were captured at Aywaille and revealed the plan. Accordingly, the general was removed from his quarters at the Trianon Palace Hotel in Versailles and kept in guarded seclusion from 19–28 December 1944 as 44 German troops clothed in British and American uniforms crossed the front lines. The three prisoners were executed by a U.S. 1st Army firing squad at Henri-Chapelle in Belgium on 23 December. Of all the infiltrators, only eight survived, 16 were executed and the remainder killed in action. The principal group leader, Günther Schulz, was tried and executed in June 1945, when he was shot at Braunschewig by the U.S. 9th Army.

At the end of hostilities Skorzeny surrendered to the U.S. Army in Bavaria and after having been detained for two years, he was put on trial at

ABOVE: At the end of the war Skorzeny surrendered to the U.S. Army, was acquitted of war crimes, and escaped Allied custody.

Dachau in August 1947, together with nine of his GREIF officers, on charges of abusing the rules of war by deploying his troops in enemy uniform. His defence was that he had instructed his men to change out of their fake uniforms once they engaged in combat, and the tribunal ruled that the tactic as described was an acceptable deception ruse. However, Skorzeny remained in detention after his acquittal, and then escaped in July 1948, marching out of his camp in an American uniform. He subsequently moved to a farm in County Kildare, and then to Madrid, where he ran an engineering business, and died in July 1975, aged 67.

An unapologetic Nazi who was also skilled in irregular warfare and the leadership of troops, Skorzeny was a swashbuckling adventurer who undertook high-risk assignments that brought him decorations, and the gratitude and admiration of his Führer.

UNCONVENTIONAL WARFARE

The contentious strategy of GREIF was typical of Skorzeny's enthusiastic adoption of unconventional warfare. This had been shown before in September 1943 with the daring rescue by glider-borne troops of Benito Mussolini from Gran Sasso high in the Apennines. Codenamed OAK, the deposed Fascist leader had been released from his confinement at the Campo Imperatore, an isolated, inaccessible mountaintop hotel, and flown to Germany to be greeted by Hitler. Skorzeny had also abducted the son of the Hungarian dictator Admiral Miklos Horthy in October 1944 in Budapest to force his abdication as regent.

ABOVE: Benito Mussolini is rescued from his mountain-top captivity by Skorzeny and his glider-borne elite troops.

PART 4

THE COLD WAR

28. CODENAME CORBY

THE DEFECTION OF IGOR GOUZENKO

CIPHER CLERK AND DEFECTOR

A 26-year-old GRU cipher clerk based at the Soviet embassy in Ottawa, Igor Gouzenko was scheduled to return to Moscow in September 1945 at the end of a tour lasting three years. However, he decided to stay in Canada with his wife, Svetlana, and his daughter, and over a period of weeks he smuggled documents from the closely guarded *referentura* in which he worked to give himself something to bargain with. In total, he removed from the building and hid in his home 109 items, which included copies of telegrams to Moscow and file entries relating to individual NKVD and GRU sources. Within the Western Alliance Gouzenko was codenamed CORBY because many of his papers in the Department of External Affairs had been stored in a cardboard box bearing the label of the Corby brand of rye whiskey.

As soon as the Soviets realized Gouzenko had gone missing they broke into his apartment and reported to the Canadian authorities that he was wanted for the theft of money. Belatedly the Canadian government realized Gouzenko's value and he was granted full protection. The implications of the material he had purloined were far reaching: the atomic scientist Alan Nunn May was identified as a Soviet spy and in February 1946 more than a dozen others were arrested and accused of supplying secrets to the Russians. They were: two engineers working for the National Research Council, Edward Mazerall and Philip Durnford Smith, and Dr Raymond Boyer, the National Research Council's explosives expert; Squadron Leader Fred Poland of the Royal Canadian Air Force; Lieutenant David Shugar, a naval radar specialist; J. Scott Benning

LEFT: The Soviet embassy in Ottawa where Igor Gouzenko worked in the GRU *referentura* as a code clerk for the *rezident*, Colonel Nikolai Zabotin.

OPPOSITE: When interviewed by the media, Gouzenko was anxious to conceal his appearance.

from the Department of Munitions and Supply; Captain David Lunan of the Canadian Army; Professor Israel Halperin, a speech-writer, and Emma Woikin, a code clerk, both in the Department of External Affairs; Eric Adams, an economist with the National Selective Service and Kay Willsher of the British High Commission. As Gouzenko named others whose cryptonyms appeared in the stolen documents, more arrests were made and the suspects were taken to the barracks of the training division of the Royal Canadian Mounted Police (RCMP) at Rockcliffe for interrogation.

The next to be detained was Harold Gerson, who was J. Scott Benning's brother-in-law and who also worked in the Department of Munitions. Squadron Leader Matt S. Nightingale, a telephone specialist, was arrested soon afterwards, under similar conditions of great secrecy to avoid tipping off other members of the Soviet network, and no public announcement was made for nearly three weeks while the Royal Commission cross-examined the detainees.

Some of the suspects were easily identified from Gouzenko's documents, while the true names of others had been protected by codenames. One vital Soviet source, codenamed ALEK, was described as a scientist at the Chalk River atomic research facility who was about to return to England to take up an appointment at London University. This was clearly a reference to the physicist Alan May, who did fly home in September, only to be arrested on 6 March 1946.

ABOVE: Fred Rose (right) the Polish-born Communist
Member of Parliament who went on the run to avoid
arrest after Gouzenko's defection.

Under interrogation, May confirmed every detail about his case already disclosed by Gouzenko and was sentenced to 10 years' imprisonment. Of the original 13 arrests, two suspects had evaded the RCMP. Fred Rose, the Communist MP for the Cartier Division of Montreal who had been on the first list of arrests was not caught until 14 March, when he was surprised at his apartment. Sam Carr, the secretary of the Communist Party had disappeared and was believed to have escaped abroad. He was not caught until January 1949, when he was arrested in New York and sentenced to six years' imprisonment.

Rose and his mistress Freda Linton were revealed as vital links between the Canadian sources and Zabotin, who handled the GRU network in Canada. Rose was identified by the British High Commissioner's secretary, Kay Willsher as her recruiter, while Freda, who had recently worked for the Film Board of Canada, apparently had acted as a go-between for Rose and Professor Boyer, an academic from McGill University who had researched the development of high explosive. Similarly David Lunan, the Scottish-born army officer who edited the military journal *Canadian Affairs*, supervised Durnford Smith, Mazerall and Halperin, and reported to Major Rogov, Zabotin's air attaché.

Some of those arrested gave detailed statements and both implicated other conspirators and served to give added credibility to Gouzenko. Kay Willsher, working in the British High Commission, named her contacts as Fred Rose and a Bank of Canada official, Eric Adams. Similarly, Emma Woikin, a clerk in the Department of External Affairs, admitted that she had routinely left secret documents in a hiding place where they were collected by Zabotin's driver, Captain Gorshkov. She had also been in close contact with the wife of the assistant military attaché, Major Vsevolod Sokolov, and had even requested Soviet citizenship. Lunan's evidence to the Royal Commission not only incriminated

himself, but compromised Halperin, Mazerall and Durnford Smith. However, in the subsequent trials, Halperin, Adams and another Bank of Canada employee, Agatha Chapman, pleaded not guilty and were acquitted.

The Royal Commission also reported that five Soviet cryptonyms, all members of Zabotin's GRU ring, had not been positively identified. They were GALYA (a housewife living next to Major Sokolov), GINI (the Jewish owner of a drugstore and a photographic laboratory), GOLIA (a young artist in a photographic studio), GREEN (an assistant to a superintendent dealing with procurement contracts in a tank assembly plant), all in Montreal, and SURENSEN, a source in naval intelligence who was believed to be Lieutenant Henning I. Sorensen, who gave evidence to the Royal Commission on a voluntary basis.

Nine of those sentenced to terms of imprisonment were either of Polish or of Russian origin and had arrived in Canada decades earlier as immigrants.

Gouzenko's testimony, combined with his stolen papers, revealed no fewer than four separate Soviet intelligence networks operating in Canada, two of which extended to the United States where the defector identified Elizabeth Bentley in Washington, DC, and Anatoli Yakovlev, based in the New York consulate, as key organizers. Vitali Pavlov was the NKVD *rezident*, with Zabotin as his GRU counterpart. A naval intelligence network had operated in Halifax and Vancouver, masterminded by a Captain Patzerney from New York but, according to Gouzenko, two other diplomats at the embassy in Ottawa undertook an intelligence function: the commercial counsellor Ivan Krotov and the second secretary, Goussarov, who headed the political section.

Gouzenko enjoyed his newfound fame and courted publicity. He sold interviews to magazines, appeared on television with a pillowcase over his head, and even sold the movie rights to his story, *The Iron Curtain*, to Twentieth Century Fox. However,

his RCMP bodyguards found him difficult to handle. With the help of his RCMP interpreter, Mervyn Black, and journalists, John Dalrymple and Laurie McKechnie, he wrote a novel, *Fall of a Titan*, and an autobiography, *This Was my Choice*, which were bestsellers. His wife also wrote a book, *Before Igor*.

In terms of the damage Gouzenko inflicted, he wrecked an organization that had taken years to develop, exposed the penetration of the Manhattan Project to develop atomic weapons and demonstrated the very close relationship between the Canadian Communist Party and Moscow.

In 1955 Gouzenko volunteered testimony to the U.S. Senate Committee on the Judiciary and was provided with the identity of a Canadian of Ukrainian extraction who had been born near Saskatoon in Saskatchewan. He lived off his royalties and a generous government pension and died at his home outside Toronto in June 1982, blinded by a combination of diabetes and alcohol.

Gouzenko's information led to the arrest of 21 who were charged, and prosecutions followed in 15 of the cases; and 12 convictions were obtained. Charges against Captain Jack Gottheil and Freda

Chalfont St. Peter. December 30th. I952

Statement to the Press Association.

I.   I do not wish to discuss the details of the action which led to
my imprisonment. I myself think that I acted rightly and I believe
many others think so too.

To those who think otherwise I would like to point out that I have
suffered the punishment which was inflicted on me by the law and
I hope I shall now be entitled to at least the consideration
normally granted to released convicts; an opportunity to restart
life.

2.   There is just one of many erroneous statements of fact which have
been made about me which I should like to correct now.

I was not convicted of treason, nor was this word used by
the prosecution or judge at my trial and I certainly had
no treasonable intentions.

I was wholeheartedly concerned with securing victory over
Nazi Germany and Japan and with the furtherance of the
developement of the peaceful uses of atomic energy in
this country.

3.   My object now is to obtain as soon as possible an opportunity
of doing useful scientific work in which I can be of some
service to this country and to my fellow men.

4.   Now that my imprisonment is over I can only wish for the same
consideration and fair treatment which I received throughout
the long period of my sentence from the prison officials and
my fellow prisoners.

Signed.

DNMay

(NO FURTHER STATEMENT WILL BE MADE OR INTERVIEWS GIVEN.)

OPPOSITE: Dr Alan Nunn May, the Cambridge-educated physicist and GRU spy codenamed ALEK who was incriminated by documents removed from the *referentura* by Gouzenko.

RIGHT: Dr May's signed statement issued upon his release from prison in December 1952.

Linton were withdrawn. Norman Veall, who had worked with Alan Nunn May at Cambridge, also escaped a charge. According to Gouzenko's documents, he had asked May's advice about passing information from the Chalk River atomic research facility to the Soviets but had been advised against such a move. When Major Samuel Burman was cross-examined, he simply denied that he was the individual referred to in a lengthy signal from Colonel Piotr Motinov to Moscow concerning one of Fred Rose's sources known as "Berman" so he was not charged. In the case of J. Scott Benning, his conviction was quashed on appeal. His only link to the ring was an entry in one of his own notebooks listing two of Fred Rose's telephone numbers in Ottawa, and an entry on a card index under the codename FOSTER, which suggested Benning had been supplying war production data to Nikolai Zheveinov, one of the TASS (Russian) news agency correspondents in Ottawa.

29. CODENAME VENONA

THE ANGLO-AMERICAN ATTACK

ON SOVIET CIPHERS

DATABASE OF SECRET INFORMATION

The arbitrarily chosen codeword, given in 1961 to the greatest secret of the Cold War, VENONA represented a collection of more than 2,000 partly decrypted Soviet secret messages and, as an authentic glimpse into the clandestine activities of the NKVD and the GRU, was more highly prized than any other comparable asset. VENONA, also known as BRIDE, SUEDE and DRUG at various different times, was limited in nature, covering communications to and from Moscow between 1940 and 1948. It represented only a tiny fraction of the traffic that was exchanged between individual diplomatic missions abroad and what was referred to as "the Centre".

VENONA

~~TOP SECRET~~

D615

USSR

Ref. No.: 3/NBF/T1971

Issued : ● /25/11/1970

Copy No.: 301

REISSUE OF ITEM 4 OF 3/NBF/T22
(of 16/1/1951)

1. FARISH, COVERNAME ATTILA; KhAZAR' AND KOLO
2. REST'S SISTER AND GUS'
3. ZORA'S TRANSFER FROM UGRYuMYJ TO KhIMIK
(1944)

From: NEW YORK

To: MOSCOW   4th October 1944

No: 1397

To VIKTOR[i].

Reference your No. 4502[a]. information, FARISH[FER'Z'][iii] (ATTILA) is in EUROPE at the present time. He is a parachutist in [C% the COUNTRY's[STRANA]][iv] Army [and][b] recently met KOLO[v]. KhAZAR received from him [4 groups unrecovered] [D% fragmentary excerpts from] a newspaper.

No. 794

[Continued overleaf]

3/NBF/T1971

VENONA

~~TOP SECRET~~

~~TOP SECRET~~

     – 2 –   3/NBF/T1971

REST's[vi] sister[vii] has not yet returned home. It is planned that GUS'[viii] should make his next trip to see her on 12th October.

No. 795

Sanction ZORA's[ix] transfer from UGRYuMYJ[x] - who is unsuitable - to KhIMIK[xi]. Details later.

No. 796   MAJ[xii]
4th October

Notes: [a] Not available.

      [b] Inserted by translator.

Comments: [i] VIKTOR: Lt. Gen. P.M. FITIN.

      [ii] KhAZAR: Unidentified covername.

      [iii] FARISH: Presumably Linn Markley FARISH, senior US Liaison Officer at TITO's HQ from September 1943; parachutist; killed 9th September 1944.

      [iv] COUNTRY: USA.

      [v] KOLO: Sava N. KOSANOVIC'; Minister in the Yugoslav Government-in-Exile.

      [vi] REST: Dr. Emil Julius Klaus FUCHS.

      [vii] REST's sister: Kristal Fuchs HEINEMAN.

      [viii] GUS':   i.e. "GOOSE"; Harry GOLD.

      [ix] ZORA: Flora Don WOVSCHIN.

      [x] UGRYuMYJ: i.e. "SULLEN"; possibly Viktor KIRILLOV.

      [xi] KhIMIK: i.e. "CHEMIST"; probably Ivan Afimovich KAMENEV.

      [xii] MAJ: i.e. "MAY"; Stepan Zakharovich APRESYaN, Soviet Vice-Consul in NEW YORK.

3/NBF/T1971

VENONA

~~TOP SECRET~~

OPPOSITE: Arlington Hall, the former girls school just outside Washington, DC, where the first cryptanalytical breakthroughs were made while studying "the Russian problem".

ABOVE: VENONA decrypt of a message sent to General Fitin from the New York *rezident*, Stepan Apresyan, dated October 1944 and mentioning Klaus Fuchs and two spies in OSS.

ABOVE: Robert Lamphere and Hugh Clegg, the FBI officers sent to London to interrogate Klaus Fuchs and identify his contacts in the United States.

Nevertheless, cryptographers in Great Britain and the United States continued to study the material until 1977, some 34 years after the U.S. Army's Signal Security Agency began work on what was then termed "the Russian problem". In the end, 2,200 individual messages were translated, but judging from their serial numbers, this was only a small proportion of the total number of Soviet communications, amounting to just under half of the NKVD's New York–Moscow circuit in 1944, 15 per cent of the 1943 traffic (about 200 out of 1,300), and only 23 of the estimated 1,300 telegrams sent in 1942, only 1.8 per cent of the total. As for the Naval GRU, half was recovered from the 1943 Washington–Moscow channel, but none for any other year. In 1940, for instance, the New York GRU is calculated to have sent 992 messages to Moscow, with 335 from the NKVD.

VENONA was rightly regarded by the very few counter-intelligence experts indoctrinated into the programme as the holy grail, a vast database of incredibly secret information that provided clues to the identities of thousands of Soviet spies across the globe. Thousands of cryptographic hours and millions of dollars were devoted to accessing an espionage mother lode, which proved to be the catalyst for hundreds of investigations across the globe, some successful, many less so. When combined with other intelligence information, known as collateral, the bare bones of a VENONA text could be enhanced by the use of footnotes. Often the collateral took the form of surveillance records, and it was physical observation that helped the FBI to work out the senior personalities operating under diplomatic cover in Washington, DC, San Francisco and elsewhere.

One example of this was when it was noted that one of the doormen at the Soviet consulate, who was known to participate in counter-surveillance operations, showed unusual deference to a particular, but relatively junior, vice consul. In fact, Stepan Apresyan was the local NKVD *rezident*, a

figure with a greater status than even the consul-general, and his wife Aleksandra was also a senior NKVD officer, codenamed ZOYA.

As a direct consequence of hints gleaned from the often-fragmented texts, Ethel and Julius Rosenberg died in the electric chair, Alger Hiss and Harry Dexter White were accused of being NKVD agents, Klaus Fuchs (see pages 164–69) was imprisoned, Donald Maclean defected and Ian Milne, an Australian diplomat, fled to Czechoslovakia.

The cryptanalytic work on VENONA was considered so secret that the Central Intelligence Agency (CIA) was only told of its existence in 1952. Each time a significant new word was decrypted in a text, or additional "collateral" had been acquired, the individual text would be recirculated to the handful of security officials who had been allowed to learn about what amounted to the most important code-breaking exercise since ULTRA. While testimony from a handful of Soviet defectors, such as Walter Krivitsky, Victor Kravchenko, Igor Gouzenko and Vladimir Petrov, added flesh to VENONA's bones, more collateral came from disaffected members of the Soviet apparatus in the United States. Whittaker Chambers, Hede Massing and Elizabeth Bentley achieved considerable notoriety for their denunciations of former comrades, and their Congressional evidence was seized on by politicians of all persuasions. The left condemned an unprincipled witch hunt of loyal civil servants; the right demanded a purge of traitors who had penetrated deep into the administration. Alger Hiss proclaimed his innocence, and Laurence Duggan committed suicide.

VENONA offered the MI5 and FBI molehunters a fascinating insight into the way the Soviets ran their intelligence operations, but the Americans took a rather more sanguine line on the dangers of hostile penetration of the government bureaucracy and, in 1954, reduced their commitment to BRIDE, a reflection of the difficulty of keeping people working on the same challenging problem for years on end.

ABOVE: Meredith Gardner, the cryptographer who solved the Japanese weather codes before devoting his life, until his retirement in 1972, to the VENONA project.

Certainly, the loss of Oliver Kirby and Cecil Phillips was a setback, as was the retirement from the FBI of Robert Lamphere in July 1955.

In contrast, senior management at GCHQ remained convinced there was plenty of scope for progress, and this turned out to be true when, in 1957, the naval attaché channel between Washington and Moscow succumbed. GCHQ was also always conscious of the NKVD and GRU spies mentioned in the early London traffic and was particularly concerned about the possibility of a traitor inside GCHQ in Eastcote itself, apparently codenamed BARON. He was mentioned in association with two other GRU spies, INTELLIGENSIA and NOBILITY, later identified as Professor J.B.S. Haldane and the Hon. Ivor Montagu, respectively.

The cause of this long-term anxiety, which was fully justified, centred on a single VENONA text dated May 1941, but broken in 1962. It quite clearly was a raw ULTRA intercept from Bletchley Park, listing the railway stations across the Ukraine that the German armoured divisions intended to utilize in the forthcoming BARBAROSSA offensive. The certainty that there was a spy inside or close to Bletchley Park in May 1941 was traumatic for two reasons. Firstly, the most obvious candidate for a traitor at Bletchley was John Cairncross, who became an espionage suspect in 1951 and was the subject of a lengthy MI5 investigation. Although he was eventually to confess to having passed his NKVD contacts thousands of ULTRA decrypts, he had not arrived at Bletchley until a year after the VENONA text. Secondly, had that person received promotion to a position where he or she could influence GCHQ's recruitment and arrange for another spy to be inserted? When the BRIDE team realized the implications, Nigel de Grey, one of the century's great cryptographers, who had solved German problems in both world wars, gathered the

staff in the Eastcote lounge and delivered a chilling lecture on the probability of a Soviet spy at large in the building.

Both Kim Philby and Anthony Blunt knew about GCHQ's work on BRIDE, but there was very little that either could do to prevent the progress made jointly at Eastcote and Arlington Hall. With his more direct access, particularly while he was MI6's liaison officer in Washington, DC, from 1949 onwards, Philby could monitor events and keep his fellow conspirators informed, but it was too late for the Soviets to repair their flawed cipher systems.

The NKVD learned as early as 1944 that BRIDE had been initiated, for in April that year a directive, intended to enhance the system's security (while achieving exactly the reverse), was suddenly circulated to all *rezidents*. Unusually, the intended change was notified by message and not in a couriered instruction, as might have been expected, and became operational at very short notice, on 1 May. The new arrangement eliminated the identification in clear of the relevant one-time pad's page number, known as the "indicator", and substituted a procedure in which the first five-digit group of the page was used in clear, to become the indicator, leaving the recipherment to begin with the second group on the page. This supposed improvement only changed the starting point by one group, and actually made the task of the cryptanalyst easier as it dispensed with the time-consuming necessity of matching page numbers to particular sections of 60 numeric groups. Instead, the attack could be concentrated on comparing the new indicators on vulnerable texts to those already thought to have been duplicated.

The VENONA project was also disclosed to Moscow by a mole in the Armed Forces Security Agency, William Weisband, probably in 1947, and then by Kim Philby in September 1949.

30. KLAUS FUCHS

THE SOVIET NETWORK IN THE MANHATTAN PROJECT

ATOMIC SPY

Klaus Fuchs was a German senior physicist based at the atomic research establishment at Harwell in Oxfordshire. In 1949 he was identified in the VENONA traffic as an NKVD spy codenamed REST and CHARLES. He was persuaded to confess to having passed secrets from Los Alamos National Laboratory to the Soviets during the war and was formally arrested in London on 3 February 1950.

Fuchs had been identified as the spy codenamed REST by an FBI special agent, Lish Whitson. In September 1949, with help from Arlington Hall cryptographers, Whitson had narrowed the field to Fuchs because of a single VENONA text. This was dated 15 June 1944 and referred to an Atomic Energy Commission document MSN-12, entitled "Fluctuations and the Efficiency of a Diffusion Plant". Part III referred to "The Effect of Fluctuations in the Flow of N2". The designation MSN indicated documents prepared by British scientists who were in New York City working on atomic energy research known as the Manhattan Project. The author of this document was Fuchs.

The incriminating VENONA text indicated that the spy had a sister in the United States. The FBI learned that Fuchs's sister, Kristel Heinemann, lived in Cambridge, Massachusetts.

Fuchs's espionage dated back to early 1941, but two years later the NKVD's London *resident*, Konstantin M. Kukin, reported to Moscow that when checking a list received from Professor Engelbert Broda, an Austrian scientist codenamed ERIC, of people working on the atomic bomb project, his attention had been drawn to Klaus Fuchs, a refugee who unexpectedly turned out to be a member of a German Communist Party underground cell. According to ERIC, Fuchs was working on rapid neutrons at Birmingham University, and when the *resident* investigated, he learned that Fuchs was known to Jurgen Kuczynski, the émigré German Communist Party leader (see pages 82–85). Kuczynski, who was not a formal agent, categorically refused to talk about Fuchs and behaved so strangely that it was concluded that he knew Fuchs was working for the Soviets. This had prompted Kukin to ask Moscow to check on Fuchs. This inquiry, at the end of November 1943, revealed that Fuchs had been a GRU agent since August 1941, when he had been approached on Kuczynski's recommendation through the Soviet ambassador Ivan Maisky.

According to the GRU file on Fuchs, Maisky was not on good terms with the NKVD *resident* Ivan Chichayev, so he had passed on Kuczynski's information to the GRU *resident* Colonel Ivan Sklyarov. He sent his secretary, Semyon Kremer, to meet Fuchs. Maisky introduced Kuczynski to Kremer, who arranged to meet Fuchs with him in a quiet side street.

At the rendezvous Fuchs told Kremer that work on building the atomic bomb had started in the United States and Great Britain. Asked by Kremer why he had decided to disclose this information, he replied that it was imperative for the Soviet Union to have its own bomb to ensure its own security.

At his next meeting with Kremer, again on a quiet London street, Fuchs handed him a large notebook with information on the British Directorate of Tube Alloys project, for the most part his own research

ABOVE: Klaus Fuchs, the first Soviet spy to be prosecuted after he had been compromised by references in the VENONA traffic to REST and CHARLES.

ABOVE: The experimental atomic pile at Harwell, the post-war centre of British nuclear research where Klaus Fuchs headed the Theoretical Physics Department.

OPPOSITE: Harry Gold, the Swiss-born chemist who had engaged in industrial espionage before the war and as identified as GOOSE in the VENONA decrypts.

Having lost touch with Kremer, Fuchs made a second approach to Kuczynski, who this time put him in touch with his sister, Ursula Beurton (see pages 82–85). She and Fuchs had their first meeting in October 1942, with his first two reports reaching Moscow on 22 and 30 September 1941. Fuchs became active again in May 1943 and gave information to Beurton on four more occasions that year, until his departure for America in November, which she passed on to the *rezidentura* through Nikolai Aptekar, codenamed SERGEI, the military attaché's driver. In Moscow, his material was handled by the NKVD's Directorate S, and specifically by three senior officers, Makhnev, Zaveniagin and Zenov.

Fuchs received his U.S. visa on 22 November 1943, and on the same day met Beurton to tell her he was going to America. At their next encounter she briefed him on how to get in touch with his American contact, "Raymond", in New York on the first Sunday in February 1944.

Once he arrived in the United States, on 7 December 1943, the responsibility for handling Fuchs passed from the GRU to Semyon Semyonov of the NKVD's New York *rezidentura*, who deployed Harry Gold as a courier and intermediary, but the two men were unable to meet until 5 February 1944. A further meeting followed on 9 February, mentioned in a VENONA cable from Leonid Kvasnikov, addressed to General Pavel Fitin.

Gold met Fuchs for a third time on Madison Avenue on 25 February, and again on 11 March in Woodside, Queens, when the physicist handed over 50 pages of information about the Manhattan Project. At this meeting, Fuchs complained about unnecessary duplication, as he had already given the same information to the GRU in England.

There was another meeting, on 28 March in Central Park, and thereafter Gold's regular fortnightly meetings with Fuchs continued uninterrupted in Brooklyn's Borough Hill Park, although the New York *rezidentura* was concerned

notes, and copies of reports and papers he had written. Kremer took it all back to the *rezidentura*, and it was sent to Moscow by diplomatic bag. The response was a cable ordering contact with Fuchs to be maintained. However, in the spring of 1942 contact was lost, partly because of a conflict that had broken out between the GRU and NKVD *rezidenturas*. Kremer was caught up in the infighting and was openly threatened by one of the NKVD staff, so he wangled himself a rapid transfer back to Moscow.

about the attention that Kvasnikov and Semyonov had attracted from the FBI. On 8 May 1944, the New York *rezident* Stepan Apresyan described how Fuchs had revealed a policy disagreement between the British and American scientists on the future of the weapons development programme.

The next month, on 15 June, Apresyan expanded on the crisis that Fuchs claimed had hit inter-Allied relations on the project, and this was followed by another telegram discussing a payment for Fuchs. However, the *rezident* never got the chance to pay Fuchs, for neither his cut-out Harry Gold, nor his new

handler, Anatoli A. Yatskov, alias Anatoli Yakovlev, codenamed ALEKSEI, had managed to make contact as scheduled on 5 August. Apresyan explained the situation in a message to Moscow on 29 August 1944, in which he gave an account of Gold's mission to find Fuchs and his visit to his sister.

A telegram from Moscow on 16 November 1944 showed that Gold (now referred to as ARNO, following a comprehensive change in codenames) had discovered that Fuchs (now known as CHARLES) had not gone to England, as had been anticipated, but had been transferred to New

ABOVE: MI5's interrogator Jim Skardon with Special Branch's George Smith at Fuchs' committal hearing at Bow Street Magistrates Court in London in February 1950.

Mexico. On 27 February 1945, Moscow asked the New York *rezidentura* for details of Fuchs's work in Chicago, and on 31 March, Moscow noted Fuchs's value, referring specifically to the Manhattan Project's K-25 gaseous diffusion plant at Clinton, Tennessee.

Evidently, in March and April 1945 the New York *rezidentura* was receiving detailed, valuable information from from the young physicist Ted Hall and Klaus Fuchs from Los Alamos, among others, at a critical moment in the development of the bomb. Tremendous progress had been made on the electric detonator, designed to initiate simultaneous explosions within a millionth of a second, and the Hanford facility on the Columbia River in Washington had reported that major deliveries of plutonium

would begin in May. Accordingly, the pressure from Moscow to cultivate new sources became intense.

When his name was passed by the FBI's Lish Whitson to MI5 in London, Fuchs was placed under surveillance. While under observation, Fuchs did nothing to incriminate himself, apart from conducting a desultory affair with Erna Skinner, the German-born wife of his neighbour and colleague.

While MI5 was contemplating the most appropriate method of approaching him, Fuchs unexpectedly visited Harwell's security officer, Henry Arnold, to disclose that his father had recently accepted a post at Leipzig University, in the Soviet zone in Germany. This coincidence gave MI5 the pretext to send its interrogator, Jim Skardon, to interview Fuchs. Their three lengthy, ostensibly informal conversations resulted in the physicist's tentative, partial admission that he had been in touch with the Soviets during the war. The result of this breakthrough was an invitation to Fuchs to attend a couple of further interviews in London, where he was arrested on 2 February 1950. On 1 March, he pleaded guilty to breaches of the Official Secrets Act and was sentenced to the maximum term of 14 years' imprisonment. In his confession, he identified Harry Gold as his Soviet contact in New York and pointed him out in a photograph during an interview conducted by the FBI at Wormwood Scrubs prison after his conviction. Fuchs not only cooperated with his interrogators, but also identified a colleague, Ronald W. Gurney, as a security risk. Gurney and his wife were investigated, and although no direct evidence of espionage was ever found, his subsequent career was blighted by the accusation.

Fuchs was released from Wakefield prison in 1959 and was deported to East Germany, where he was appointed director of the nuclear research establishment at Dresden and a member of the Central Committee. He married a former fellow student at the University of Kiel and died in January 1988, aged 76.

ABOVE: FBI Director J. Edgar Hoover briefs the press after receiving the news of Fuchs' arrest in London.

THE FUCHS MYSTERY

One enduring mystery concerning Fuchs was a contact in London with whom he communicated by tossing a magazine into a garden in Richmond, west London. Fuchs had been told to use a dead-letter box at 166 Kew Road, where he was instructed to throw a copy of *Men Only* onto the garden lawn with his message written on page 10. The occupants were known CPGB members: Charles Moody, who had been implicated in the Woolwich Arsenal case in 1938, his wife Gerty and her sister Claire Isaacs. The latter pair had been in trouble for distributing subversive anti-war literature to troops in 1935. All three suspects were interviewed by MI5's interrogator, Jim Skardon, but they denied any knowledge of Fuchs's drop arrangements, so this aspect of the case remained unresolved. Moody, however, had accumulated a large MI5 file dating back to August 1931 and had been linked in the past to George Aitken, the CPGB's propaganda director who had attended the Lenin School in Moscow in 1927 and served as the political commissar to the XVth International Brigade during the Spanish Civil War.

31. THE CAMBRIDGE RING OF FIVE

SOVIET AGENTS INSIDE THE BRITISH ESTABLISHMENT

MOLEHUNT

The term "Ring of Five" was originally coined by Anatoli Golitsyn, a defector from the Soviet intelligence agency, the KGB, who was granted asylum in the United States in December 1961, having deserted the KGB *rezidentura* in Helsinki. He claimed that there had been five Soviet spies in England, all young men who had known each other and who had been recruited before the war, probably while at the same university.

Suspicion immediately centred on the diplomats Guy Burgess and Donald Maclean, who had both fled to the Soviet Union in May 1951. At the time, Maclean had been under intense surveillance, having been compromised by VENONA decrypts, and was days away from being called in for questioning by MI5, but Burgess had not been investigated. Their sudden disappearance had served to implicate Kim Philby, then MI6 liaison officer in Washington, DC, who had been dismissed from his post in June 1951. Although the subject of an interrogation in the following December, Philby had protested his innocence and denied having tipped off Maclean by sending a warning to him through Burgess. His performance fooled nobody present at the encounter, but in the absence of any firm evidence that could be adduced in a criminal court, he was free to take up his old profession, that of journalism.

The defection of Burgess and Maclean had also incriminated Anthony Blunt, the art historian and former wartime MI5 officer known to be close to Burgess and Philby, but over 13 interviews he would persist in denying his involvement. His apparently distinguished career as Surveyor of the Queen's Pictures was rewarded in 1956 with a knighthood, an award that suggested that he was an utterly loyal servant of the crown.

However, documents found in Burgess's London flat compromised another Cambridge graduate, John Cairncross, who was obliged to resign his post at the Treasury in April 1952, and he then moved to Rome. Although he had denied having spied, his MI5 interrogator was convinced of his guilt. Since his recruitment in 1936 he had served in no fewer than six Whitehall departments.

At the time of Golitsyn's disclosures, only Burgess and Maclean – who eventually had surfaced in Moscow in February 1956, but not made any admissions beyond confirming their political conversion to Communism – had been confirmed as traitors. The search for the third, then fourth and fifth men would continue until April 1982 when Cairncross publicly acknowledged his treachery.

The idea that anyone would deliberately, willingly betray their country and adhere to a foreign dictatorship was an alien concept. The five men, all Cambridge graduates, had relatively privileged backgrounds and had gained significant positions of trust within government service. All had enjoyed access to highly sensitive Whitehall information, ranging from Cairncross's role in drafting a cabinet report detailing the development of atomic weapons, to Blunt's supervision of some

OPPOSITE: Guy Burgess, the predatory homosexual who advised MI6 on broadcasting, ran agents for MI5 during the war and then joined the Foreign Office.

ABOVE: Kim Philby, the Soviet spy recruited in 1934 who would eventually confess
to his espionage in January 1963, in return for an immunity from prosecution.

extremely delicate MI5 operations, and his wartime responsibility for assembling MI5's monthly reports to the prime minister.

By the time Golitsyn revealed his knowledge of the Ring of Five, the members were all known to MI5, but his information prompted further inquiries which led to an offer of immunity made to Philby, then living in the Lebanon, in return for a confession and his full cooperation. MI5 had come to the conclusion that in the absence of concrete proof, and no prospect of a successful conviction, the leverage of immunity represented a potentially powerful and persuasive method of gaining useful information.

ABOVE: Anthony Blunt (left) spent decades at the heart of the establishment and was Surveyor of the Queen's Pictures. Donald Maclean (right), the son of a Cabinet minister, was the first of the Five to gain access to classified information.

Philby, employed as a journalist by the *Observer* and the *Economist*, accepted the terms, supplying a three-page statement in which he admitted his commitment to the Soviets since 1934, but a few days later, in January 1963, he disappeared from his Beirut apartment. Upon close examination, his confession turned out to be carefully crafted lies.

In February 1964 Cairncross was re-interviewed by Arthur Martin, an MI5 molehunter who travelled

ABOVE: Trinity College, Cambridge, where Kim Philby returned a year after his graduation to recruit his friend Guy Burgess, who then recruited others.

to see him in the United States, and on this occasion he admitted his recruitment at Trinity College by James Klugmann, a well-known Communist who had been appointed the Party's official historian. During the same journey, while staying at the home of the FBI's Bill Sullivan, the MI5 officer met another Cambridge graduate, Michael Whitney Straight, who was the wealthy proprietor of *New Republic* magazine. He also acknowledged having been recruited while a student, and named Blunt as the

person responsible. Upon his return to Washington, DC, Straight had joined the U.S. State Department and passed classified material to his Soviet handler but insisted he had broken off contact later in the war.

In April 1964 Blunt, confronted by MI5's Arthur Martin with Straight's allegation, accepted an immunity from prosecution that had been negotiated with the attorney-general, Sir John Hobson, and, over the following 15 years gave a detailed account

of the activities of the Ring of Five and identified others on the fringes of the group who had acted as sub-agents. Among them was Leo Long, a wartime MI14 analyst; James MacGibbon; an MI3 officer who had served in Washington, DC; the Welsh academic Goronwy Rees; Henry Smollett of the Ministry of Information, and others who had merely flirted with Communism. As Golitsyn had correctly suggested, the original Ring of Five had grown in size.

During the war the Ring of Five had penetrated almost every secret branch of the British government, including MI5, MI6, Bletchley Park, the War Office, the Foreign Office, the Ministry of Information and the Cabinet Office. After the war its members haemorrhaged secrets from the Foreign Office, MI6, the Treasury, the Control Commission for Germany and the Ministry of Supply. None was ever prosecuted. Burgess, Maclean and Philby died in Moscow; Blunt and Cairncross died in England.

32. PROJECT SHAMROCK

THE INTERCEPTION OF INTERNATIONAL
CABLE TRAFFIC

INTERNATIONAL EAVESDROPPING

At the end of the Second World War the U.S. Department of Defense was persuaded by the Army Security Agency (ASA) to approach the three biggest U.S.-based international commercial carriers, RCA Global, ITT World Communications and Western Union, to copy all their private and commercial traffic and supply it to the ASA. This procedure was in violation of the provisions of the 1934 Federal Communications Act, relevant to

ABOVE: Seal of the U.S. National Security Agency.

BELOW: A telegraph switchboard.

OPPOSITE: Fort George C. Meade in Mayland, headquarters of the National Security Agency

domestic wiretapping, but the ASA had assured the senior management of the companies concerned, in 1947 and again in 1949, that there was no chance of prosecution, and that anyway the law was open to several different interpretations if the intercepted traffic was to, or from, an overseas destination.

The issue at stake was the requirement to obtain a court-approved warrant to intercept the domestic communications of U.S. citizens, but the law had been passed at a time when there was limited overseas telephone traffic, and the principal targets were chiefly foreign entities, individuals and organizations, whose traffic had a potential intelligence value. As it was explained to the cable companies, a public law specifically authorizing the measures could be put before Congress, but such a strategy would serve to alert potential adversaries. In 1952, when the National Security Agency (NSA) was created, it simply inherited this project, named SHAMROCK, and in the years that followed enhanced it, first at the request of the U.S. Secret Service which asked, in the aftermath of John F. Kennedy's

ABOVE: RAF Menwith Hill in Yorkshire, a component of the worldwide network of satellite ground-stations that gives the National Security Agency (NSA) access to international communications.

assassination, for certain political extremists to be targeted, and then in response to the Pentagon, which was suspicious of foreign involvement in the anti-Vietnam War protesters. By 1971 the Secret Service's list had grown to 180 Americans considered a potential risk to the president, and 825 foreign organizations. In addition, the CIA Counter-Intelligence Staff and Office of Security added their own targets for investigation, as had the Bureau of Narcotics and Dangerous Drugs. Physically, the duplicate tapes were collected from each of the company headquarters daily by two officials, one an FBI special agent, the other from the NSA, and taken to a covert site in lower Manhattan managed by the CIA with the codename LP/MEDLEY.

In 1967 Lyndon B. Johnson's administration authorized another extension of SHAMROCK to cover American domestic traffic and, in particular, communications to and from names on a list of civil rights and anti-war activists compiled by the FBI. Eventually the watch-list would grow to 1,000 Americans, with a further 1,700 foreigners and overseas groups. Within the NSA this potentially illegal project was codenamed MINARET and was put into operation with passive assistance from the NSA's British partner, GCHQ.

At that time most of America's overseas communications were routed across the Atlantic via one of two Intelsat satellites in permanent geosynchronous high orbit, 36,000 kilometres (22,375 miles) over the ocean. The ground bases for the transatlantic traffic were located at Andover, Maine, and Etam, West Virginia, on America's eastern seaboard, and at Madley in Herefordshire and Goonhilly in Cornwall in the British Isles. Each of the two satellites could handle up to 4,000 telephone circuits and rather more telex or data channels. By the end of 1967, the NSA had secretly constructed two identical receiving stations at Winter Harbor, Maine, and Sugar Grove, West Virginia. Coincidentally, two similar bases were built in England, at Menwith Hill in Yorkshire and

at Morwenstow in north Cornwall. The first site, an area of windswept Yorkshire moorland outside the market town of Harrogate, had been occupied by the ASA's 13th Field Station since 1955, although it only came under the NSA's direct control in August 1966. The second, on the cliffs above the seaside village of Morwenstow, was within GCHQ's Composite Signals Organization.

By initiating the MINARET programme on British territory, the NSA hoped to avoid a breach of the 1934 statute. The problem had arisen with the passage of the 1968 Omnibus Crime Control Act, which had introduced restrictions on wiretaps, and established a requirement to obtain a warrant. One way to circumvent the U.S. legislation was to undertake the actual interception of long-distance traffic in a foreign jurisdiction, such as the United Kingdom.

Once intercepted, the resulting product (which required no decryption as it was generally in plain language) was relayed via a secure NSA channel to Fort Meade for processing by an IBM 7090 computer, which boasted a capacity of 230,000 separate calculations per second. However, the project was to be short-lived, for the NSA ceased taking "nominations" (additions to the list of names they were following) from other agencies in September 1972, and MINARET was finally abandoned in May 1975, in the wake of the Watergate investigations of 1973 and the numerous Congressional inquiries into contentious intelligence collection operations. A few years earlier, in 1969, ITT had dropped out of the arrangement, and had so informed the Pentagon, and the FBI had withdrawn in October 1972, while simultaneously questioning the legality of the Secret Service's watch-list.

Despite the fragility of the legal status surrounding SHAMROCK and MINARET, some aspects of the telephone intercept project survived until at least January 1976, as part of the CIA's counter-intelligence operation codenamed MN/CHAOS which was supposedly intended to monitor Soviet efforts to tap into American telephone

circuits. According to the NSA's testimony to the Senate Intelligence Committee, a total of just over 3,900 MINARET reports had been compiled by the NSA on American citizens during 1975.

MN/CHAOS, staffed by 42 CIA officers operating from basement offices in the headquarters building at Langley, obtained some of its material from the NSA, but most came either from the FBI or from its own resources, a group of fewer than 30 agents who were infiltrated, mainly in Europe, into dissident

ABOVE: James Angleton, Chief of Counterintelligence at the CIA, who appeared to testify to the Church committee in June 1975 that intelligence officers should lie to Congress to protect secrets.

extremist groups which advocated violence, such as the Black Panthers. Ironically, MN/CHAOS lasted much longer than expected because the Johnson White House was unwilling to accept the verdict that there was no evidence of foreign intelligence funding for the activists.

33. OPERATION PIMLICO

THE EXFILTRATION FROM MOSCOW
OF OLEG GORDIEVSKY

KGB MOLE

A member of the KGB's Third Department, First Chief Directorate, Line PR, specializing in political reporting, Oleg Gordievsky was recruited in Copenhagen in 1974 by the MI6 station commander, Robert Browning, with the help of the Danish security police, the PET.

Although initially reluctant to accept Gordievsky, who was considered rather too good to be true, MI6's management came to accept his reports as genuine, and while still in Denmark he was able to compromise several local KGB assets, including the Danish journalist Arne Petersen, the Norwegian diplomat Arne Treholt and a Norwegian Foreign Ministry secretary, Gunvor Haavik. However, when he was recalled to Moscow in 1978 he fell silent, and did not resume contact until June 1982, when he was posted to the London *rezidentura*, then headed by Arkadi Gouk.

Once established in London, Gordievsky met his new MI6 handler, John Scarlett, contact having been made via a dedicated telephone number which he had memorized four years earlier. After the KGB officer called the number a rendezvous had been made in a hotel in Sloane Street; Gordievsky had ducked out of the rear of the hotel, into Pavilion Road, to be driven to a safe-house in Bayswater, where he had been introduced to Scarlett. Later, Gordievsky was given the front-door key to a flat close to the embassy to which he could disappear with his family should the need ever arise.

Ten months after his arrival in London, Gordievsky was placed in jeopardy in a potentially massive

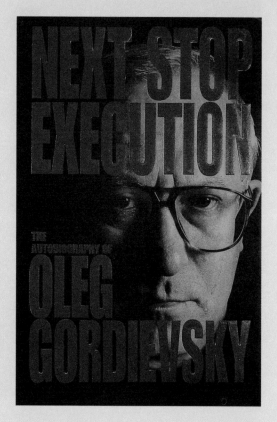

breach of MI5's own security when a middle-ranking officer, Michael Bettaney, attempted to pass secret documents to Gouk. Naturally, Gouk consulted Gordievsky about the anonymous, gratuitous offer, and was advised that the material

ABOVE: Gordievsky's controversial memoirs *Next Stop Execution* in which he named four Labour MPs as "confidential contacts" of the KGB *rezidentura*.

OPPOSITE: Oleg Gordievsky, soon after his exfiltration from Moscow in July 1985, wearing a false beard.

was probably a deliberate provocation and should best be ignored. Gordievsky then tipped off his MI6 handler to the danger, and the errant Bettaney, who had joined MI5 eight years earlier, was arrested and imprisoned.

It was during this final period of Gordievsky's highly productive period as an agent that he provided the most valuable political reporting of his career. He had returned to the West fully briefed from the First Chief Directorate headquarters at Yasenevo in Russia, and had been ideally placed to give crucial help to NATO in interpreting the tumultuous events taking place in Mikhail Gorbachev's politburo, the policy-making committee of the Communist Party.

On Friday, 17 May 1985, having been named the *rezident* designate, Gordievsky was unexpectedly summoned home to Moscow, supposedly for consultations, but he was very suspicious and only agreed when he had been assured by MI6 at an emergency meeting that there was no reason to believe he was in any danger. However, upon his arrival he realized his apartment had been searched, and when he reached Yasenevo he was accused of being a spy. He denied the accusation and resisted his interrogators, who used drugs in an attempt to extract a confession, but he concluded that although the KGB had been tipped off to his dual role, there was not sufficient evidence to justify an arrest.

Although under heavy surveillance, Gordievsky was able to shake off his watchers while jogging in a park at the end of July and make contact with MI6. He sent an emergency signal requesting a rescue, which was promptly relayed to London. The seemingly innocuous signal was nothing more elaborate than Gordievsky appearing on a prearranged street corner, at a particular time, carrying a shopping bag. This apparently innocent act prompted the UK Foreign Office secretary,

LEFT: Fort Monckton, near Gosport, MI6's training facility on the Solent where Gordievsky was accommodated while he was debriefed in 1985.

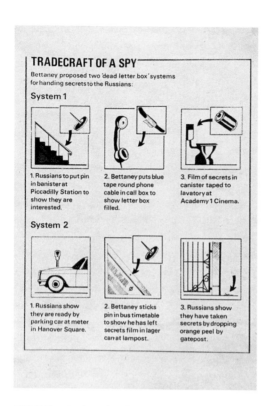

TRADECRAFT OF A SPY

Bettaney proposed two 'dead letter box' systems for handing secrets to the Russians:

System 1

1. Russians to put pin in banister at Piccadilly Station to show they are interested.

2. Bettaney puts blue tape round phone cable in call box to show letter box filled.

3. Film of secrets in canister taped to lavatory at Academy 1 Cinema.

System 2

1. Russians show they are ready by parking car at meter in Hanover Square.

2. Bettaney sticks pin in bus timetable to show he has left secrets film in lager can at lampost.

3. Russians show they have taken secrets by dropping orange peel by gatepost.

ABOVE: The classic tradecraft of signal-sites and dead-drops suggested by MI5 traitor Michael Bettaney.

ABOVE: Prime Minister Margaret Thatcher personally authorized Gordievsky's high-risk exfiltration from Moscow while she was staying with the Queen at Balmoral.

Charles Powell, to fly to Scotland immediately to brief Prime Minister Margaret Thatcher, who was staying with the Queen at Balmoral, while Foreign Secretary Geoffrey Howe was visited at Chevening. When informed of the need for their permission to undertake the perilous act of removing Gordievsky from Moscow over the weekend under the noses of the KGB who were maintaining a watch on him, both approved the submission.

Arrangements, codenamed PIMLICO, were made for Gordievsky to be exfiltrated by the Moscow station commander, Viscount Asquith, in his Vauxhall Viva car to Finland. Asquith posed as a Samaritan, supposedly escorting a pregnant member of the embassy staff for medical treatment in Helsinki, while Gordievsky climbed aboard at a rendezvous outside Leningrad and was driven over

the frontier at Viborg. Once in Finland Gordievsky was driven to Norway for a flight the next day from Oslo to London and then accommodated briefly at a country house, South Ormsby Hall, in Lincolnshire. He was visited there by MI6 chief, Christopher Curwen.

After a few days' of rest, Gordievsky was transferred to Fort Monckton in Hampshire for a lengthy debriefing, lasting 80 days, conducted by MI6's principal Kremlinologist, Gordon Barrass. Although he had never served behind the Iron Curtain, Barrass had served on the Joint Intelligence Committee's Assessment Staff before becoming MI6's expert on the Soviet collapse. Among Gordievsky's other visitors was the director of U.S. Central Intelligence, Bill Casey, who was flown down to the fort for a lunch hosted by Curwen.

Although Gordievsky's safe exfiltration was a source of great pride and celebration, there remained considerable concern about precisely how he had been compromised. One possibility was that after so many losses, the KGB had worked out for itself that a mole had been at work within the organization. As well as tipping off MI6 to Bettaney and the spies in Norway, Gordievsky had been responsible for the arrests in Denmark of a journalist, Arne Herlov Petersen who had been an agent of influence since his recruitment in 1973 by Leonid Marakov, later the *rezident* in Oslo. Petersen had penetrated the Danish peace movement for the KGB and had been arrested in November 1981, but was released without charge. In contrast, a Danish businessman, Bent Weibel, also in the pay of the KGB and responsible for smuggling high-tech equipment to Moscow, was convicted with espionage and sentenced to eight years' imprisonment. Quite apart from these two cases of espionage, the KGB had also suffered an unprecedented seven expulsions of diplomats from the embassy.

It was not until the arrest of the CIA's Aldrich Ames in February 1994 that it was suspected he had identified Gordievsky to the Soviets as a source codenamed AE/TICKLE who had penetrated the KGB in Denmark and London. Ames admitted responsibility for betraying a dozen other assets in the Soviet Union, but it was how the KGB had latched on to Gordievsky that had so preoccupied MI6. When debriefed, Gordievsky was emphatic that his KGB interrogators had been sure of his guilt, but without the proof required to make an arrest, and his recall had been a consequence of his identity becoming known in Moscow.

Between the successful exfiltration in August 1985 and the arrest of Ames eight and a half years later, MI6 was tormented by the fear that their own ranks had been penetrated by a mole. The identification of Ames appeared to lay those fears to rest – even if Gordievsky had in the meantime struck up a professional relationship with the counter-intelligence expert – until the CIA expressed some doubt about whether the dates matched. Gordievsky had flown to Moscow on Sunday 19 May, having been recalled two days earlier, but in his sworn testimony Ames insisted that he had not betrayed Gordievsky until the following month, when he had met his controller, Viktor Cherkashin, on 13 June. Ames admitted having passed over the names of two FBI assets inside the Soviet embassy in Washington, DC, Sergei Motorin and Valeri Martinov, as his initial offer on 16 April, but insisted that he had not included Gordievsky on that occasion. Nor had he mentioned him when he had picked up his payment from Cherkashin on 15 May. The mystery remains unresolved.

Gordievsky was resettled under a new identity near London, and eventually reunited in November 1991 with his wife Leila and two daughters Anna and Maria. He later divorced, and subsequently lived with an English public school matron. In 1994 wrote his memoirs, *Next Stop Execution*. As well as describing his role in compromising the KGB's spies in Norway and Sweden, Gordievsky revealed that the KGB *rezidentura* had run a *Guardian* journalist, Richard Gott, as a paid agent of influence, and had taken steps to cultivate several highly placed trade union leaders, among them Richard Briginshaw, Ray Buckton and Alan Safer. Gordievsky claimed that the embassy was also in touch with what he termed "confidential contacts", influential individuals who could be relied upon to take the Kremlin's lead on political controversies. These included three left-wing Labour MPs, Joan Lester, Jo Richardson and Joan Maynard. Others implicated by Gordievsky included two editors of *Tribune*, Michael Foot and Dick Clements.

The constitutional implications of Gordievsky's disclosures were considered sufficiently important for Curwen to brief Cabinet Secretary Sir Robin Butler, who in turn called in Tony Blair, as leader of the opposition.

PART 5

THE
MODERN ERA

34. OPERATION NEPTUNE SPEAR

THE ASSASSINATION OF OSAMA BIN LADEN

HUNT FOR THE MOST WANTED

Al-Qaeda ("The Base") was created in Saudi Arabia in 1992 by Osama bin Laden, a Wahhabi adherent who opposed the deployment of U.S. forces in his country after the Iraqi occupation of Kuwait. It was intended to protect Islam's holy places from defilement by foreigners. Bin Laden, previously a supporter of the mujahideen in Afghanistan, was exiled to Sudan by the Saudi government, where he planned a jihad or holy war against the United States. This manifested itself in a series of attacks on the U.S. embassies in Nairobi, Kenya, and Dar es Salaam, Tanzania, in August 1998 and an attempt to sink the USS *Cole* in Aden in October 2000. On 11 September 2001 bin Laden masterminded the coordinated hijacking by 19 terrorists of four U.S. passenger aircraft from Boston, Newark and Washington, DC, two of which crashed into World Trade Center in New York and a third into the Pentagon. In the four years following the 9/11 attacks, al-Qaeda was responsible for bomb atrocities in Bali, Madrid, Casablanca, Istanbul, Sharm el-Sheikh and London and was linked to other attacks that were thwarted.

In February 1992 American-led coalition forces occupied Afghanistan in an effort to remove the Sunni fundamentalist Taliban from power in Kabul, eliminate al-Qaeda training camps and decapitate the organization's headquarters in the Tora Bora mountains. The operation was largely successful, with the capture of numerous detainees who were flown to Cuba for interrogation at the U.S. naval base at Guantanamo Bay. Interference with al-Qaeda's communications and financial support network led bin Laden to adopt a "franchise" strategy,

TOP: The emblem of the U.S. Navy SEALS.

ABOVE: Osama bin Laden, the Saudi-born Islamic cleric whose message of *jihad* inspired a generation of al-Qaeda terrorists.

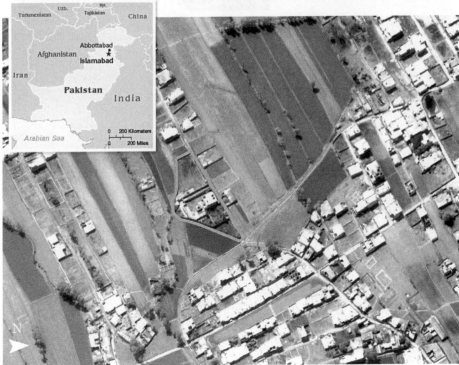

TOP: A ground view of the unusually high wall protecting the bin Laden compound in Abbottabad, Pakistan.

ABOVE: Overhead imagery of Osama Bin Laden's walled compound in Abbottabad.

Most Wanted Terrorists

MURDER OF U.S. NATIONALS OUTSIDE THE UNITED STATES;
CONSPIRACY TO MURDER U.S. NATIONALS OUTSIDE THE UNITED STATES;
ATTACK ON A FEDERAL FACILITY RESULTING IN DEATH

USAMA BIN LADEN

Aliases: Usama Bin Muhammad Bin Ladin, Shaykh Usama Bin Ladin, the Prince, the Emir, Abu Abdallah, Mujahid Shaykh, Hajj, the Director

DESCRIPTION

Date of Birth Used:	1957	**Hair:**	Brown
Place of Birth:	Saudi Arabia	**Eyes:**	Brown
Height:	6'4" to 6'6"	**Sex:**	Male
Weight:	Approximately 160 pounds	**Complexion:**	Olive
Build:	Thin	**Citizenship:**	Saudi Arabian
Language:	Arabic (probably Pashtu)		
Scars and Marks:	None known		
Remarks:	Bin Laden is believed to be in Afghanistan. He is left-handed and walks with a cane.		

CAUTION

USAMA BIN LADEN IS WANTED IN CONNECTION WITH THE AUGUST 7, 1998, BOMBINGS OF THE UNITED STATES EMBASSIES IN DAR ES SALAAM, TANZANIA, AND NAIROBI, KENYA. THESE ATTACKS KILLED OVER 200 PEOPLE. IN ADDITION, BIN LADEN IS A SUSPECT IN OTHER TERRORIST ATTACKS THROUGHOUT THE WORLD.

REWARD

The Rewards For Justice Program, United States Department of State, is offering a reward of up to $5 million for information leading directly to the apprehension or conviction of Usama Bin Laden. An additional $2 million is being offered through a program developed and funded by the Airline Pilots Association and the Air Transport Association.

SHOULD BE CONSIDERED ARMED AND DANGEROUS

IF YOU HAVE ANY INFORMATION CONCERNING THIS PERSON, PLEASE CONTACT YOUR LOCAL FBI OFFICE OR THE NEAREST AMERICAN EMBASSY OR CONSULATE.

www.fbi.gov

October 2001

ABOVE: The U.S. Department of Justice-approved poster designed to encourage informers.

OPPOSITE: A Black Hawk gunship similar to the aircraft deployed during the raid. One crashed and was destroyed to prevent recovery of the secret engine noise suppression system.

sponsoring disparate terrorist groups across the globe and offering them bomb-making expertise and advice on tactics. He offered minimal financial aid, leaving the terrorists to raise cash through credit card fraud and other criminal activity.

The CIA's ALEC station, a headquarters unit dedicated to tracing bin Laden, found him on ten occasions during the Bill Clinton administration, but each time the White House refused permission for his assassination. Specifically, plans were drawn up in 1996 and again in 1997 when bin Laden had been traced to Tarnak Farms, his training camp near Kandahar. The project included intervention by local tribes that had been put on the CIA's payroll, but the Pentagon sought to include a parachute drop involving 300 Special Forces. Eventually the White House vetoed the proposal on the grounds that the civilian collateral damage might result in a bloodbath among the 19 women and children bin Laden was known to surround himself with.

A further opportunity presented itself in February 1999 when bin Laden received a visit from a member of a royal family in one of the United Arab Emirates (UAE). The prince's arrival on a C-130, part of the UAE's royal flight, was monitored by the CIA but another proposal to launch a missile attack during the entourage's evening meal, shared with bin Laden before prayers, was rejected for fear of offending the Gulf states. Significantly, none of the ALEC station plans had been supported by Director of Central Intelligence George Tenet. Frustrated, the ALEC station chief, Michael Scheuer, circulated a memorandum listing how the CIA needed to respond to the al-Qaeda challenge. However, in June 1999 he was transferred by Tenet's deputy, Jack Downing, to a cubicle in the CIA's library and replaced by Richard Blee. An unarmed CIA drone took video footage of bin Laden on 7 September 2000.

The information that led the CIA to bin Laden's two trusted couriers, who used the aliases Ibrahim

LEFT: President Obama, Secretary of State Hillary Clinton and the national security team in the White House Situation Room watching a live relay of bin Laden take-down.

BELOW: The USS *Carl Vinson* which deployed Prowler EA-8 electronic warfare aircraft to jam Pakistan's ground defences during the SEAL Team Six operation.

OPPOSITE: A SEAL Team Six member undergoes routine live-fire combat training.

and Abrar Ahmed al-Kuwaiti, originated with the interrogation of Khalid Sheikh Mohammed, who was captured in Rawalpindi in March 2003. Having been waterboarded at a CIA black site, he cooperated with his interrogators and provided a wealth of information about al-Qaeda. The other source was another high-value detainee, Abu Faraj al-Libi, a Libyan who was seized by Pakistan's Inter-Services Intelligence in Mardan in May 2005 and was subjected to enhanced interrogation techniques.

Other arrests followed, including members of bin Laden's personal support group, consisting of Abu Musaab al Balochi, Umar Kathio alias Abdullah Al-Sindhi, Amal Ahmed Abul Fateh, Mustafa Muhammad Khan alias Hassan Gul, Ramzan alias Abu Harith, Ammar Chottu and Dr Akmal Waheed, who were all caught between 2004 and 2006. The

leads provided by them eventually resulted in the identification of the al-Kuwaiti brothers, who were then placed under surveillance and watched as they visited bin Laden's heavily protected compound.

Thereafter a CIA operation, which included a bogus vaccination programme conducted by a Pakistani physician, Dr Shakeel Afridi, to trace the DNA of bin Laden's children, sought unsuccessfully to verify the terrorist's presence in the compound. Once confirmation had been obtained, Operation NEPTUNE SPEAR was initiated, which consisted of an intense training programme at a CIA compound at Harvey Point, North Carolina, where a replica building was constructed.

Bin Laden eventually was killed by Robert J. O'Neill in a 40-minute firefight with 24 members of U.S. Navy SEAL Team Six personnel on 1 May

2011 in a large, fortified compound in Abbottabad, 60 kilometres (35 miles) from Islamabad, a site that had been monitored 24 hours a day for eight months. Bin Laden was found to have been living in a large, three-storey mansion built in 2005 that, very curiously, did not appear to have either telephone or internet access, nor require any rubbish collection. The Special Forces were deployed from Bagram air base in Afghanistan after months of training in two Black Hawk helicopters, and a pair of Chinooks.

Also killed at the scene were three men, one thought to be bin Laden's 19-year-old son Khalid.

Bin Laden's 29-year-old wife Khalifa was wounded in the leg. Recovered from the building were several laptops, memory sticks, mobile phones and satellite phones, which underwent forensic examination, and a large quantity of manuscript notes. Bin Laden's body was transported to the carrier USS *Carl Vinson*, and buried at sea. Under interrogation, Khalifa disclosed that her husband had not left his suite of rooms for five years, and had taken refuge for two years in a remote Pakistani village before moving to the purpose-built house, which also accommodated nine other women and 15 children.

NAVY SEALS

Known officially as the Naval Special Warfare Development Group (DEVGRU), the U.S. Navy SEALS are an elite Special Forces unit within the Joint Special Operations Command that was formed in 1979. Consisting of 1,300 counter-terrorism specialists, it is divided into six colour-coded assault squadrons, and based at the Coronado, in San Diego, California. DEVGRU personnel are trained in amphibious warfare to exacting standards and have been deployed across the globe, most recently in Afghanistan, Iraq, Mali and the Philippines.

35. THE SKRIPALS AND JAMAL KHASHOGGI

THE FUTURE OF COVERT OPERATIONS

ENEMIES OF THE STATE?

Abduction, murder and torture are usually the desperate hallmarks of failing regimes headed by despots. In recent years there has been a distinct trend of incidents of violence perpetrated against individuals perceived as enemies of the state.

The attempt on the life of Colonel Sergei Skripal, a GRU officer and convicted spy, who was attacked with the lethal toxin Novichok at his home in Salisbury in the UK in March 2018, was probably an act of retribution committed by his former comrades in the Russian military intelligence service whom he had betrayed. Freed halfway through a 13-year prison sentence in Russia as part of a spy exchange involving the release of ten Directorate S "illegals" arrested in the United States, Skripal was resettled in England under his own name.

OPPOSITE: Police seal off the house of a couple who appeared to have been accidentally poisoned by Novichok, a substance used on the Skripals some months earlier.

ABOVE: Forensic technicians in protective suits examine the area contaminated by the lethal Novichok nerve agent used to attack Colonel Skripal.

Also included in the swap were a Russian academic, Igor Sutyagin and two CIA assets, Alexander Zaphorovhsky and, more importantly, Gennadi Vasilenko. At the time the Russians had not realized the significance of Vasilenko, who had been a mole inside the KGB for years. Nor had they known that the Russian foreign intelligence service, the SVR, had been penetrated at a high level by two other agents, Aleksander Poteyev and Alexei Shcherbakov. who had been quietly exfiltrated from Moscow just before the FBI rounded up the American network.

It would be some time before the Kremlin came to understand the scale of the humiliation inflicted, but it sought revenge against Skripal, after a lengthy surveillance operation conducted by Denis Sergeev and other GRU personnel flown into England on

ABOVE: Colonel Anatoliy Chepiga and Alexander Mishkin are recorded by CCTV in Salisbury on their way to Skripal's home.

short-term assignments for the sole purpose of locating Skripal and watching his movements. Then it deployed a GRU duo, assassin Colonel Anatoliy Chepiga and his combat physician, Dr Alexander Mishkin, to administer the poison, which was smeared on the handle of Skripal's front door.

Skripal and his daughter Yulia both survived the murder bid, but others were not so lucky. The former Russian Federal Security Service officer Alexander Litvinenko, died in London in November 2006 after ingesting polonium-210, and the Bulgarian dissident broadcaster Georgi Markov succumbed two days after he had been injected with ricin on Waterloo Bridge in September 1978.

The police inquiry into Litvinenko's death named his former KGB colleague Andrei Lugovoi and Red Army soldier Dmitri Kovton as the men responsible, but both had returned to Moscow. Lugovoi's later election to the Russian Duma, giving him an immunity from prosecution, was strongly suggestive of official collusion. Similarly, Markov's killer was never caught, but Scotland Yard named

an Italian, Francesco Gullino, as having been hired by the Bulgarian agency Darzhavna Sigurost.

The common denominators of all three deaths was the use of exotic substances, which implied an element of state-sponsorship, and the active hostility of the relevant intelligence agency. Such cases are quite rare, probably because of the adverse media coverage they attract, although where a rogue nation that ignores the accepted international norms of behaviour is involved, expediency may outweigh any disadvantages. This could have been the motivation behind the abduction and murder of the Saudi journalist and *Washington Post* columnist Jamal Khashoggi, who was killed in Istanbul in October 2018 while visiting the Saudi consulate.

Allegedly Khashoggi, whose remains have not been recovered, was asphyxiated while being served tea by consular staff, and then dismembered. The episode was planned on the orders of the Saudi Crown Prince, Mohammed bin Salman, who had been the subject of Khashoggi's criticism. He

뉴스속보 北 김정남 피살
"우상화 걸림돌 제거"

연합뉴스TV

뉴스속보 양무진 북한대학원대학교 교수

23 뉴스리뷰 쿠알라룸푸르 · 자카르타 등지서 여러...

21:35   명 중 2명 "숙제 없는 학교 찬성"   ▶ 도심 차량 제한속도, 202...

OPPOSITE: The CCTV record of Sergei Skripal shopping in his local convenience store shortly before the attack.

ABOVE: TV news reports of the assassination in Kuala Lumpur of President Kim Jong-Un's half-brother, Kim Jong-Nam.

deployed a team of 15 assassins led by one of Salman's senior aides. General Maher Abdulaziz Mutreb, who previously had been posted to the Saudi embassy in London. The others were Salah Muhammed A. Tubaigy, a Glasgow University-trained forensic scientist; Major Waleed Abdullah M. Alsehri and Lieutenant Meshal Saad M. Albostani, both air force officers; a Special Forces soldier, Naif Hassan S. Alarifi; Colonel Muserref M. Alsehri, Fahad Shabib A. Albalawi, Abdulaziz Muhammed M. Alhawsawi, Abdulaziz Muhammed M. Alhawsawi and Khalid Aedh G. Alotaibi, all members of the elite Royal Guard; Colonel Mansur Othman M. Abahüseyin of the Civil Defence Corps; Mustafa Muhammed M. Almadani of the General Intelligence Directorate; one of the Crown Prince's aides, Saif Saad Q. Alqahtani; Türki Muserref M. Alsehri; and 45-year-old Badr Lafi M. Alotaibi.

All, of course, were closely associated with the regime in Riyadh and the fact that a number of them were currently serving in the Crown Prince's personal entourage or the royal bodyguard suggested a direct link between the country's political leadership and the assassination, despite denials from the Saudi government, which claimed to have arrested 18 suspects. Eleven were subsequently charged with murder, the prosecution seeking the death penalty for five of the defendants.

The investigations conducted by the Turkish police and the CIA concluded that bin Salman was personally culpable for the murder, which had been committed by assassins of whom most were employed by the Saudi *Mukhabarat*. In response the foreign minister, Adel al-Jubeir, was replaced by Ibrahim Addulaziz al-Assaf, and there was a reorganization of the intelligence service.

The willingness of some intelligence agencies to eliminate their political masters' opponents has escalated, as indicated by the murder in Malaysia of Kim Jong-Nam, the elder half-brother of the North Korean tyrant Kim Jong-Un in February 2017. Apparently viewed as a potential rival by Jong-Un, the playboy gambler was placed under surveillance by the regime as he led a sybaritic lifestyle, occasionally making public criticisms of his family.

Jong-Nam, carrying a diplomatic passport in the name of Kim Chol, had been waiting to check in for a flight to Macao at Kuala Lumpur's international airport when he was splashed in the face with VX gas by to two women. They were Doan Thi Huong, a 28 year-old Vietnamese woman, and a 25 year-old Indonesian, Siti Aisyah, who were caught on CCTV security cameras assaulting the 46 year-old Kim. He died within minutes, and his assailants later claimed to have been hired for a prank organized by a reality television show. They would both be imprisoned, but only briefly, the prosecution having accepted their version of the crime. Huong was sentenced to 40 months' imprisonment but was released in May 2019. Her companion had been set free two months earlier following intensive political lobbying from Djakarta.

ABOVE: A surveillance CCTV camera captured the moment Jamal Khashoggi entered the Saudi consulate-general on the day he was killed.

LEFT: Turkish police seal off and search the Istanbul home of the Saudi consul-general following the murder of Jamal Khashoggi.

ABOVE: Seal of the Saudi General Intelligence Service.

RIGHT: The news of Khashoggi's murder sparks international condemnation.

Outlawed internationally in 1997, VX gas was a retained by only a few countries, including North Korea, where sophisticated production and storage facilities were known to exist. The fact that most other stockpiles in the world had been destroyed under verified procedures strongly indicated state sponsorship of the murder, and this suspicion was compounded by the apparent involvement Pyongyang diplomats. Soon afterwards four Ministry of State Security officers based at the North Korean embassy fled the country.

The second secretary at the North Korean embassy, Hyon Kwang-Song, Kim Uk-Il, who was employed by Air Koryo, and a 30 year-old woman, Ru Ji-U, were identified by the Malaysian police as suspects in what was described as a political assassination orchestrated from Pyongyang. Others wanted for questioning were four North Koreans, Hong Song-Hac, Ri Ji-Hyon, O Jong-Gil, and Ri Jae-Nam who flew out of the country soon after the attack, leaving yet another manifestation of the impugnity with which

outlaw states have come to rely on intelligence professionals to cling to power.

The common denominators in these examples of modern-day abuse of power are the undemocratic and unaccountable nature of the regimes responsible and the ruthless, brazen manner in which the acts were perpetrated, apparently in flagrant disregard for international norms of behaviour. The employment of sophisticated nerve agents and toxins, or personnel closely associated with a particular government, is a strong indicator of state sponsorship and the tacit approval of the rulers confident of evading any adverse consequences. In these circumstances, when the concept of plausible deniability has been abandoned, the elimination of a political opponent, even in a foreign, potentially high-risk jurisdiction, must appear to be a very attractive expedient for the commissioner of the crime. The absence of any such calculation, weighing the advantages against a political downside, suggests a complete moral vacuum.

GLOSSARY

Abwehr	German intelligence agency
ASA	U.S. Army Security Agency
BCRA	French intelligence service
black site	Unacknowledged CIA detention facility
Cheka	Soviet intelligence service (1917–1922)
CIA	U.S. Central Intelligence Agency
CIS	Combined Intelligence Service
Comintern	Communist International
CPGB	Communist Party of Great Britain
cut-out	Intermediary
dead-drop	Clandestine message exchange site
en clair	An ordinary telegram, not in cipher
Deuxième Bureau	French military intelligence agency
FBI	U.S. Federal Bureau of Investigation
Fremde Heere	German naval intelligence service
FSB	Russian federal security service
GCHQ	British Government Communications Headquarters
GRU	Soviet (then Russian) military intelligence service
hand cipher	Non-mechanical encryption system
IRA	Irish Republican Army
ISOS	Abwehr hand cipher decrypts
ISK	Enigma machine cipher decrypts
KGB	Soviet intelligence service
konspiratsia	Soviet espionage tradecraft
KPD	German Communist Party
MI5	British security service
MI6	British secret intelligence sservice
MI-8	U.S. Army signal intelligence service
N	Nachrichtenabteilung – Imperial German navy intelligence branch
NATO	North Atlantic Treaty Organization
NKVD	Soviet intelligence service
NSA	U.S. National Security Agency
OGPU	Soviet intelligence service
OSS	Office of Strategic Services

PCO	Passport Control Office(r)
RAF	British Royal Air Force
Rezidentura	Premises of the Soviet intelligence station
RIC	Royal Irish Constabulary
RSS	Radio Security Service
SD	Sicherheitsdienst – Nazi Party and SS intelligence agency
SHAEF	Supreme Headquarters Allied Expeditionary Force
SIS	U.S. Signal Intelligence Service
SOE	British Special Operations Executive
Stay-behind-network	A clandestine organization established prior to an enemy occupation, which only becomes active after the frontline has moved on.
SVR	Russian foreign intelligence service
ULTRA	Generic codename for signals intelligence derived from summaries of Axis decrypts German communications.

FURTHER READING

Accoce, Pierre, and Pierre Quet. *The Lucy Ring*. London: W. H. Allen, 1967.

Aldrich, Richard. *The Hidden Hand*. London: John Murray, 2001.

Andrew, Christopher. MI5. *The Defence of the Realm*. London; Allen Lane, 2009

Bamford, James. *Body of Secrets*. New York: Doubleday, 2001.

Barron, Robert Louis, and Michael Warner. *Venona*. Washington, D.C.: National Security Agency, 1996.

Batvinis, Ray. *The Origins of FBI counterintelligence*. (Lawrence, KS: University Press of Kansas, 2007,

Bennett, Ralph. *Ultra in the West*. London: Hutchinson, 1979.

Best, Sigismund Payne. *The Venlo Incident*. London: Hutchinson, 1950.

Black, J. L. & Martin Rudner (Eds.). *The Gouzenko Affair; Canada and the Beginnings of Cold War Counter Espionage*. Manotick, Canada: Penumbra Press, 2006

Borovik, Genrihk. *The Philby Files*. Boston: Little, Brown, 1994.

Bothwell, Robert and J.L. Granatstein (eds.). The Gouzenko Transcripts: The Evidence Presented to the Kellock Taschereau Royal Commission of 1946. Ottawa, Ontario: Deneau Publishers, 1982

Bower, Tom. *The Perfect English Spy*. London: Heinemann, 1995.

Breindel, Eric, and Herbert Romerstein. *The Venona Secret*. New York: Harper-Collins, 1999.

Costello, John. *Mask of Treachery*. London: Collins, 1988.

Cairncross, John. *The Enigma Spy*. London: Century, 1997.

Carter, Miranda. *Anthony Blunt*. New York: Farrar, Straus & Giroux, 2001.

Cave Brown, Anthony. *'C': The Biography of Sir Stewart Menzies*. London: Macmillan, 1987.

Chester, Lewis, Stephern Fay and Hugo Young. *The Zinoviev Letter*. London: Heinemann, 1967.

Cook, Andrew. On His Majesty's Secret Service: Sidney Reilly Codename ST1. Stroud, Gloucestershire: Tempus Publishing, 2002.

Cookridge, E. H. Gehlen. *Spy of the Century.* New York: Random House, 1971.

Costello, John. *Mask of Treachery.* New York: William Morrow, 1988.

Coulson, Thomas. *Mata Hari: Courtesan and Spy.* New York: Harper Publishers, 1930.

Deakin, F. W., and G. R. Storry. *The Case of Richard Sorge.* London: Chatto & Windus, 1966.

Delmer, Sefton. *Counterfeit Spy.* London: Hutchinson, 1973.

Denniston, A.G. *The Government Code and Cypher School Between the Wars.* Intelligence and National Security. Vol. 1, No. 1.

Dorril, Stephen. *MI6.* London: Fourth Estate, 2000.

Dourlein, Pieter. *Inside NORTH POLE: An Agent's Story.* London: William Kimber, 1953.

Driberg, Tom. *Guy Burgess.* London: Weidenfeld & Nicolson, 1956.

Dukes, Sir Paul. *The Story of ST-25.* London: Cassell, 1938.

Everitt, Nicholas. *British Secret Service during the Great War.* London: Hutchinson, 1920.

Fisher, John. *Gentleman Spies: Intelligence Agents in the British Empire and Beyond.* Phoenix Mill: Sutton, 2002.

Foot, M.R.D. *SOE in France.* London: HMSO, 1966.

Foot, M.R.D. *SOE in the Low Countries.* London: St Ermin's 2001.

Fourcade, Marie-Madeleine. *Noak's Ark.* London: Allen & Unwin, 1973.

Giskes, Hermann. *London Calling North Pole.* London: William Kimber, 1953.

Gordievsky, Oleg. *Last Stop Execution.* London: Macmillan, 1995.

Gouzenko, Igor. *This was my Choice: Gouzenko's Story.* London: Eyre & Spottiswoode, 1948.

Gouzenko, Svetlana. *Before Igor: My Memories of a Soviet Youth.* London: Cassell, 1961.

Haynes, John Earl, and Harvey Klehr. *Venona.* New Haven, Conn.: Yale University Press, 1999.

Hennessy, Peter. The Secret State. London: Penguin, 2002.

Hesketh, Roger. F*ORTITUDE: The D-Day Deception Campaign.* London: St Ermin's Press, 1999.

Hill, George. *Go Spy The Land.* London: Cassell, 1932.

Hinsley, F.H., with E.E. Thomas, C.F.G. Ransom and R.C.

Knight. *British Intelligence in the Second World War.* London: HMSO, 1979.

Hinsley, F.H. and Anthony Simkins. *British Intelligence in the Second World War: Security and Counter-Intelligence.* Vol. 4. London: HMSO, 1990.

Hohne, Heinz. *Codeword: DIREKTOR.* London: Secker & Warburg, 1971.

Holt, Thadeus. *The Deceivers.* London: Simon & Schuster, 2004.

Jeffery, Keith. *MI6.* London: Bloomsbury, 2010.

Judd, Alan. *The Quest for C.* London: HarperCollins, 1999.

Kahn, David. *Herbert O. Yardley and the Birth of American Codebreaking.* New Haven, CT: YUP, 2004.

Kahn, David. *Seizing the Enigma. The Race to Break the German U Boat Codes, 1939–1943* Boston: Houghton Mifflin, 1991.

Keraris, Paul, ed. *The Rote Kapelle.* Frederick, Md.: University Publications of America, 1979.

Knightley, Philip. *Philby.* London: Jonathan Cape, 1997.

Lawson, J.C. *Tales of Aegean Intrigue.* London: Chatto & Windus, 1920.

Lewin, Ronald. *Ultra Goes to War.* New York: McGraw-Hill, 1978.

Liddell, Guy. *The Guy Liddell Diaries.* London: Routledge, 2005.

Lownie, Andrew. *Stalin's Englishman; The Lives of Guy Burgess.* London; Hodder,2015

Macintyre,Ben. *The Spy and the Traitor.* London; Random House, 2018

Mackenzie, Compton. *Greek Memories.* Frederick, MD: University Publications of America, 1987.

Mackenzie, Compton. *Greek Memories.* London: Cassell, 1932.

Mackenzie, Compton. *Water on the Brain.* London: Chatto & Windus, 1933.

Mackenzie, Compton. *My Life and Times: Octave Seven.* London; Chatto & Windus, 1968.

Mackenzie, William. *The Secret History of SOE.* London: St Ermin's, 2000.

MacKinnon, Janice, and Stephen MacKinnon. *Agnes Smedley.* Berkeley: University of California Press, 1988.

Martin, John. *The Mirror Caught the Sun. Operation Anthropoid.* Liverpool; John Martin, 2009.

Mulley, Clare. *The Spy Who Loved Me.* London: Macmillan, 2012.

Masterman, J.C., *The Double Cross System of the War of 1939-45*. Boston, Mass: Yale University Press, 1972.

Matthews, Owen. *The Impeccable Spy; Richard Sorge, Stalin's Master Agent*. London: Bloomsbury, 2019.

Meissner, Hans-Otto. *The Man with Three Faces*. New York: Rinehart, 1955.

Miller, Russell. *Dusko Popov*. London: Orion, 2004.

Mitrokhin, Vasili, and Chrstopher Andrew. *The Mitrokhin Archive*. London: Penguin, 1999.

Monkhouse, Allan. *Moscow 1911-33*. London: Victor Gollancz, 1933.

Montagu, Ewen. *The Man Who Never Was*. London: 1954.

Montagu, Ewen. *Beyond Top Secret U*. London: Coward McCann, 1978.

Moss, Norman. *Klaus Fuchs*. London: Grafton Books, 1987.

Page, Bruce, Phillip Knightley, and David Leitch. *The Philby Conspiracy*. New York: Doubleday, 1968.

Peis, Gunter. *The Man Who Started the War*. London: Odhams,1960.

Penrose, Barry, and Simon Freeman. *Conspiracy of Silence*. London: Grafton, 1986.

Perrault, Gilles. *The Red Orchestra*. London: Arthur Barker, 1968.

Philby, Eleanor. *The Spy I Loved*. London: Hamish Hamilton, 1967.

Philby, H.A.R. Kim. *My Silent War*. London: MacGibbon & Kee, 1968.

Philby, Rufina, and Hayden Peake. *The Private Life of Kim Philby*. London: St. Ermin's Press, 1999.

Popov, Dusko. *SpyCounterSpy*. London: Weidenfeld & Nicolson, 1973.

Pratt, Donovan, *The Rote Kapelle The CIA's Hisotry of Soviet Intelligence and Espionage Networks in Western Europe 1936 1945*. Frederick, MD: University Publications of America, 1979.

Pujol, Juan. *GARBO*. London: Weidenfeld & Nicolson, 1985.

Purvis, Stewart, and Jeff Hulbert. *Guy Burgess: The Spy Who Knew Everyone*. London: Biteback, 2006.

Radó, Sándor. *Codename DORA*. London: Abelard, 1977.

Reese, Mary Ellen. *General Reinhard Gehlen and the CIA Connection*. Fairfax, Va.: George Mason University Press, 1990.

Reilly, Sidney. *Sidney Reilly: Britain's Master Spy*. London: Dorset Press, 1985.

Richelson, Jeffrey, and Desmond Ball. *The Ties That Bind*. Boston: Allen & Unwin. 1985.

Sawatsky, John. *Gouzenko: The Untold Story*. Toronto: Macmillan, 1984

Sawatsky, John. *Men in the Shadows. The RCMP Security Service*. Toronto: Doubleday Canada, 1980

Seale, Patrick, and Maureen McConville. *Philby*. London: Hamish Hamilton, 1973.

Seaman, Mark. *GARBO: The Spy Who Saved D-Day*. London: PRO, 2000.

Smith, Michael. *New Cloak, Old Dagger*. London: Cassell, 1996.

Stephenson, William. *British Security Coordination*. London: St. Ermin's Press, 1998.

Schellenberg, Walter. *The Labyrinth*. London: New York; Da Capo Press, 2000.

Thatcher, Margaret. *The Downing Street Years*. London: HarperCollins, 1993.

Thomaselli, P. *C's Moscow Station – The Anglo-Russian Trade Mission as a Cover for SIS in the Early 1920s*. Intelligence and National Security. Vol, 17, No. 3.

Trevor Roper, Hugh. *The Philby Affair*. London: William Kimber, 1968.

Urban, Mark. *The Skripal Files*. London; Macmillan,2018.

Weinstein, Allen, and Alexander Vassiliev. *The Haunted Wood*. New York: Random House, 1999.

Werner, Ruth. *Sonia's Report*. London: Chatto & Windus, 1991.

Wheatley, Dennis. *The Deception Planners*. London: Hutchinson, 1980.

Williams, Robert Chadwell. *Klaus Fuchs, Atom Spy*. Cambridge, Mass.: Harvard University Press, 1987.

Willoughby, Charles. *Shanghai Conspiracy*. New York: E. P. Dutton, 1952.

Whymant, Robert. *Stalin's Spy*. London: I. B. Tauris, 1996.

Wilson, Owen. *Murder in Istanbul*. London; Gibsin Square, 2019

Winterbotham, Frederick. *The Ultra Secret*. London: Weidenfeld & Nicolson, 1974.

Woodhall, Edwin. *Spies of the Great War*. London: Mellifont Press, 1933.

Wright, Peter. *SpyCatcher*. New York: Doubleday, 1987.

INDEX

PICTURE CREDITS

CHAPTER OPENER CAPTIONS

Page 6: Invasion beach in southern France on 15 1944. Allied assault troops from landing craft advance through a breach in a defence wall.

Pages 8–9: Combat ready special operation forces soldiers in the water with automatic rifles.

Page 10: Arms allegedly found at Croke Park in Dublin after Auxilliaries opened fire at a crowded Gaelic football match.

Page 42: German forces using an Enigma machine (left) during the Second World War.

Page 64: A codebreaking machine at Bletchley Park.

Page 150: A tram leaving the American sector at Checkpoint Charlie in Berlin in the 1950s.

Page 188: A Hazmat (hazardous materials) team conducting checks inside Kuala Lumpur International Airport in February 2017 following the murder of Kim Jong Nam.

DROPPING AREA

• Le Muy

FIRST AIRBORNE
TASK FORCE

North

45 x 36

Frejus

RED
264 A

St. Aygulf Pt.

45th Division

Pt. Ale

XX
45

XXX
VI

BLUE
2630

YELLOW

GREEN
2638

Plan De La Tour

180

St. Maxim
RCT

RED
2634

263

C. Sardineau

Pte. De L'Ay

C. St. Trop

St. Pons

Golfe De St. Tropez

3 x 45

Grimaud
La Foux

262

St. Tropez

3 x 45
(Proposed for
Admin only)

Cogolin

Baie
De

Gassin

261

YELLOW

Pampelonne

XX
3

FR. COMMANDO
("ROMEO")

RED

259

260

C. Camarat

Baie de
Bon Porte

Baie De Cavalaire

C. Taillat

Baie de Briande

C. Lardier

C. Cavalaire

RENDEVOUS AREA FOR SHIPS
IN RETURN CONVOYS.

C. Negre

Rade De Bormes